Edward, Lord Herbert of Cherbury

Twayne's English Authors Series

Arthur F. Kinney, Editor

University of Massachusetts at Amherst

TEAS 439

EDWARD HERBERT
(1582–1648)
Portrait by William Larkin
Photograph courtesy of The National Trust, London

Edward, Lord Herbert of Cherbury

By Eugene D. Hill

Mount Holyoke College

Twayne Publishers
A Division of G.K. Hall & Co. • Boston

Edward, Lord Herbert of Cherbury

Eugene D. Hill

Copyright © 1987 by G.K. Hall & Co.
All Rights Reserved
Published by Twayne Publishers
A Division of G.K. Hall & Co.
70 Lincoln Street
Boston, Massachusetts 02111

Copyediting supervised by Lewis DeSimone
Book production by Marne B. Sultz
Book design by Barbara Anderson

Printed on permanent/durable acid-free paper
and bound in the United States of America

Library of Congress Cataloging in Publication Data

Hill, Eugene D.
  Edward, Lord Herbert of Cherbury.

  (Twayne's English authors series; TEAS 439)
  Bibliography: p. 134
  Includes index.
  1. Herbert of Cherbury, Edward Herbert, Baron,
1583–1648—Criticism and interpretation. I. Title. II. Series.
PR2294.H2Z68 1987   821'.4   86–19506
ISBN 0–8057–6933–1

Contents

Editor's Note

Often lost in the shadow of his younger brother, the poet George Herbert, Edward, Lord Herbert of Cherbury, was a vastly better known writer in his own time and is still an important figure in the history of English thought and literature. As philosophy, his famous work *De Veritate* made him "the father of English deism" and the most important English forerunner of the Enlightenment; as biography and history, his *Life and Reign of King Henry the Eighth* has been placed alongside Bacon's life of Henry VII as one of the classic English works of Tudor history; his "Ode upon a Question moved," according to a scholar of the period, "bears comparison with the most beautiful poems in English literature," while his frank autobiography, published posthumously, is, according to Swinburne, one of the hundred best books ever written. Lord Herbert's poetry, moreover, shows a unique development of Donne's philosophy and Marino's imagery and tone, thus forging a new sort of metaphysical poetry in English in the seventeenth century. Now, in a new and comprehensive study of the man and his work, which draws with a penetrating acuity on the best and most recent English and European scholarship, Eugene D. Hill shows how all of Herbert's career—both his successes and his failures in the world of politics, philosophy, and poetry—is united in his understanding and promulgation of deist thought. Since such ideas were often considered heretical and punishable by death, Lord Herbert developed his own poetics of "double-voiced" works, a technique "of purposeful obliquity that Herbert learned in his diplomatic career." Lord Herbert's thought and literary work have been difficult and obscure for far too long; Professor Hill, at last, untangles the recalcitrant prose and poetry revealing works of provocative thought and unusual beauty in a study for Twayne's English Authors Series that rescues one of the finest talents of the English seventeenth century.

—Arthur F. Kinney

About the Author

Educated at Stuyvesant High School in New York City and at Columbia College, Eugene D. Hill was a Kellett Fellow at Balliol College (Oxford) before taking his doctorate in English at Princeton University. His writing has appeared in *Modern Philology, Shakespeare Quarterly,* and *English Literary Renaissance,* among other journals. He is currently doing research on Milton and the baroque vision of politics and is an associate professor of English at Mount Holyoke College.

Dr. Hill spent the 1984–85 academic year at the University of Pittsburgh as a Mellon Research Fellow; much of this book was written at that time.

Preface

Edward, Lord Herbert of Cherbury (ca. 1582–1648) would have been astonished if he could have foreseen the eventual eclipse of his reputation by that of his younger brother, the devotional poet George Herbert. The latter died in 1633 a "country parson," his poems mostly unpublished. But Edward Herbert was in his own day a man of renown. Distinguished as philosopher, poet, and historian, Herbert also played a notable role on the European scene as British ambassador to France in the difficult period that witnessed the outbreak of the Thirty Years War. His contemporaries were generous in their judgment of Herbert's gifts. As early as 1616, Ben Jonson professed not to know what to praise first, asking

> If men get name, for some one virtue: Then,
> What man art thou, that art so many men,
> All-virtuous HERBERT! on whose every part
> *Truth* might spend all her voice, *Fame* all her art.
> Whether thy learning they would take, or wit,
> Or valour, or thy judgement seasoning it.[1]

In the seventeenth century, even hostile commentators took Herbert seriously. The German scholar Christian Kortholt gave Herbert pride (or infamy) of place in his book *Three Great Impostors* (1680). Attacking Herbert, Hobbes, and Spinoza as an unholy trio of hypocrites who strove to undermine the Christian religion, Kortholt devoted his longest chapter to Lord Herbert's philosophy of religion.[2] And in the next century, Voltaire, the most brilliant of polemicists against institutional religion, made much the same point as Kortholt. Of course the Frenchman admired what the German had abhorred: as Voltaire wrote in 1767, Herbert was "one of the first" of those "who had the daring to stand up, not only against the Roman Church, but against the Christian Church."[3]

Like him or loathe him, eighteenth-century commentators agreed on Herbert's significance. As John Leland wrote in 1754, Lord Herbert was "the most eminent of the deistical writers." By deism Leland understood, rightly, the rejection of revealed religion in general, and of Christianity in particular, in favor of a universal "natural" creed accessible to all men.[4]

But in the nineteenth and twentieth centuries, Herbert has faded from view. To be sure, he is mentioned in all the reference books and receives perfunctory treatment in all the literary histories and histories of philosophy that cover the early seventeenth century. But though often mentioned, he is rarely discussed. The Modern Language Association Bibliography for 1983 records no entries for Lord Herbert, as against some three dozen for George Herbert.

Why Herbert has been so neglected is less easy to say. A fine German historian of English deism contended that the English were too tied to religion and to religious factions to do justice to the deist movement. That was in a book published in 1841.[5] More recently, one might suspect, deism has seemed old hat, a forgotten stage in the history of rationalism. Deism might appear of interest mainly to students of the American and French Revolutionary period, when it enjoyed the adherence of figures as different as Robespierre, Jefferson, and Ethan Allen. (The Green Mountain Boy was a fervent polemicist in the deist cause.)

Even a late nineteenth-century agnostic like Leslie Stephen — a gifted historian of thought as well as Virginia Woolf's father — had little patience with the early deists. It is notorious that he belittles their argumentation as against that of their orthodox Christian opponents. One scholar has suggested that Stephen was irked with the early deists because flaws in their arguments left debating points open for the orthodox opponents Stephen shared with the deists.[6]

In an essay on Lord Herbert published in 1900, Stephen goes out of his way to disparage his subject as a dilettante, whose admitted versatility led him to "squander his powers." Stephen cannot manage a favorable word for any of Herbert's books. And he writes that Herbert's "vanity implies a deficient sense of humour, but nobody who reads his works will be surprised at that." Stephen also avers that "the singular self-conceit of the autobiography is not that of a strong man."[7]

Stephen's essay has set the pattern for much of the twentieth-century scholarship. Mario Rossi's massive three-volume study fills in the details with impeccable erudition.[8] But Rossi's view of Herbert remains precisely the same as Stephen's. And one can suspect that Rossi's tomes have done more to discourage work on Herbert than any other factor. Apart from the obstacle of 1,600 pages of Italian, the study seemed to suggest that (1) Rossi had said what needed to be said and (2) the subject was of little interest to begin with.

Rossi's bias against Herbert and everything he stood for could not be more patent. Rossi was an outstanding scholar, justly praised by Yeats as "this profound critic of philosophy, this scholar learned in all the schools who can make himself intelligible to the running man."[9] Rossi was, however, committed to the view that a philosophy of religion was an impossibility, religion being a matter of faith. This is a defensible view with a long tradition behind it. But it could not fail to inhibit Rossi's sympathy for Lord Herbert's work. One can cite Rossi's own remarks in a volume he published in English, *A Plea for Man* (1956). "Biography has a religious purport"; it "gives pause to our pride before God." Rossi insists that his biographical works "should be considered not as historical monographies but as explorations in the field of moral philosophy." Rossi could not be more explicit about the "religious ideas" that "underlie" his theory of biography.[10]

It would be difficult to conceive of a less suitable guide to the works of Lord Herbert, the father of English deism, than a scholar who attributes much that he disapproves of in modern thought precisely to deism.[11] Only such a writer could conclude a study of Herbert by comparing him unfavorably with Kierkegaard, that exemplary Knight of Faith. Indeed, as a guide to Herbert's basic intention, one would do better to follow a malign seventeenth-century commentator like Kortholt, who clearly and briefly conveys the thrust of Herbert's thought and the subtlety of his polemical strategy.

The present volume will reexamine Lord Herbert from a disinterested but sympathetic perspective. Its goal is to make his writings more accessible and more attractive to the larger audience of readers that he merits. Not merely a name to be dutifully mentioned in historical overviews, Herbert is an author who should be read with the same kind of care we bring to his friends Donne and Jonson or to his younger brother George.

Where Rossi sees in Lord Herbert a mere dilettante, a well-disposed reader can see a diplomat — in his literary production as in his overseas career. Herbert's books show a consistent strategy by which he seeks to train a reader in independent judgment. Prime instruments of that training are wit and humor — in Herbert these often take the form of irony: saying less than, even the opposite of, what one means. Now irony, like humor in general, depends upon discrepant awareness, upon different degrees of understanding in one mind as against another. And so too does diplomacy. The very word *diplomat* derives from a Greek word meaning "twofold." In his writing, Herbert employs wit to create a meaningful doubleness of utterance. This procedure is the diplomat's stock in trade; Herbert applies it to philosophy and poetry as well. The present volume will show how he does so. The proof is cumulative, each chapter bringing the reader closer to a mastery of Herbert's characteristic strategy of argument and tone of address.

Chapter 1 provides a short biography of Lord Herbert. Chapter 2 takes up the intellectual and historical context of his philosophy of religion and presents an account of his first book, *De Veritate.* Chapter 3 deals with his later writings on religion. Herbert's two volumes of history provide the subject of chapter 4, especially *The Life and Reign of King Henry the Eighth,* in which Herbert applied (with masterly irony) his philosophy of history to the sixteenth-century Reformation in England. Chapter 5 introduces Herbert's poetry and explores its stylistic sources in Donne and Marino. Chapter 6 presents Herbert's poetic sequences, notably the "color" poems and the poems of Platonic love. Chapter 7 offers a full reading of Herbert's verse masterpiece, the "Ode upon a Question moved, Whether Love should continue for ever?" Chapter 8 covers the notorious autobiography, long Herbert's most widely read book. In conclusion, chapter 9 examines Herbert's critical reputation in light of his achievement as author and thinker.

Eugene D. Hill

Mount Holyoke College

Chronology

1644   Gives up Montgomery Castle to parliamentary forces
        in September.

1644   Returns to London in October.

1645   *De Religione Laici* and *De Causus Errorum*.

1648   Dies in London in August.

1649   *The Life and Reign of King Henry the Eighth*.

1656   *The Expedition to the Isle of Rhé*.

1663   *De Religione Gentilium*.

1665   *Occasional Verses*.

1764   Herbert's autobiography.

1768   *A Dialogue between a Tutor and his Pupil*.

Chapter One

Herbert's Life

The Early Years

The Herbert Family. Edward Herbert was born in Eyton-on-Severn, Shropshire, on 3 March 1582.[1] Though the Herbert family claimed descent from a companion of William the Conqueror in the eleventh century, prior to the fifteenth century they had been "small Monmouthshire gentry of little estate."[2] Between then and the time of Herbert's birth, they ascended the social ladder to become one of the leading families of Wales. They rose through faithful service to high noblemen and to the Crown, through military prowess, and through a series of judicious marriages. Around the year 1460, the family abandoned the Welsh system of patronymics for the English pattern of family surnames; thus Sir William ap Thomas was the father of William Herbert (created earl of Pembroke in 1468). The adoption of the English system was "natural enough" for a "Welsh family living on the borders of England, and seeing itself to be rising rapidly in the world."[3]

The Herberts suffered a blow during the War of the Roses, when in 1469 the earl of Pembroke and his brother Sir Richard Herbert were captured by Lancastrian rebels and beheaded. Sir Richard's son and grandson became leading agents of the Tudor Crown in consolidating its hold over mid-Wales. In return for their services, they received both land and political power. Sir Richard's grandson, the poet-philosopher's grandfather and namesake, Edward Herbert (d. 1593), became constable of Montgomery Castle, as well as proprietor of other manors, including Cherbury, or Chirbury, which lies just over the Shropshire border from Montgomery. It was his grandfather who, as Lord Herbert reports blandly in his autobiography, was so successful as courtier, soldier, and administrator that he "got so much money and wealth, as enabled him to buy the greatest part of that livelihood which is descended to me."[4]

Lord Herbert's grandfather represented the county of Montgomery in Parliament. (The family also controlled the seat for the borough

1

of Montgomery.) With only a handful of exceptions, a member of the Herbert family sat for the county in every Parliament from 1553 until the Long Parliament of 1640. Such were the prerogatives of being the principal local magnate, as both Lord Herbert and his grandfather were. Indeed, on the one occasion, in 1588, when the Herberts' control over the county seat was hotly contested, the family's supporters were ready to oblige with some electoral shenanigans to ensure the desired result. As J. E. Neale, a master of Elizabethan history, explains in a classic article on disputed elections in the period, "Play fair, play foul, in Montgomery a Herbert had to win."[5]

Education.   In the autobiography, Herbert recalls his earliest memory of childhood. "When I understood what was said by others, I did yet forbear to speak, lest I should utter something that were imperfect or impertinent." When he "came to talk," one of his first "inquiries . . . was, how I came into this world" (Lee, 15). As a toddler, it would appear, he was already a taciturn philosopher with a penchant toward deist inquiry. The autobiography contains many stories that, like this one, are best treated as components of Herbert's artful self-presentation in that book. But one must fall back on the autobiography for much of what can be known of Herbert's education.

Herbert reports that he passed the first nine years of his life at his maternal grandmother's home in Eyton. At that point he was sent to live with a tutor to learn Welsh, but the boy was too ill with a fever to pick up much Welsh. A year later he was sent to another tutor, with whom Herbert made rapid progress in Greek and logic (Lee, 20–21). From his studies, it is clear that the Herbert family had accepted the relatively new idea that the sons of the English aristocracy should be sent to university to prepare them for their destined careers in public life. And young Edward was duly matriculated as a gentleman commoner at University College in May 1596.

Herbert had been at Oxford only a few months when he was called home to be with his dying father. And soon after his return to school, negotiations began for his marriage. A young woman from another branch of the Herbert family, Mary Herbert, had been promised a large inheritance on condition that she marry a Herbert. Negotiations between her parents and Herbert's uncle went on for two years. The marriage finally took place in February 1599: the bridegroom was not quite seventeen, the bride was about twenty.

Herbert writes: "Not long after my marriage I went again to Oxford, together with my wife and mother, who took a house, and lived for some . . . time there. . . . Having a due remedy for that lasciviousness to which youth is naturally inclined, I followed my book more close than ever, in which course I continued until I attained about the age of eighteen, when my mother took a house in London, between which place and Montgomery Castle I passed my time till I came to the age of one-and-twenty, having in that space divers children" (Lee, 22–23).

Herbert's had been a marriage of convenience, so it is hardly surprising that he treats his wife, from whom he would eventually be estranged, as a mere sexual convenience. What does call for comment in the preceding quotation is the action of Herbert's mother, Magdalen Herbert, who twice transplants her residence and family (there were nine children after Edward)—to Oxford in 1599, to London in 1601. Her character is best remembered for the praise it evoked from John Donne, whom she met about this time, and from Izaak Walton, who between them lauded her piety, her charity, her hospitality, and her beauty. Both indicate that she came to Oxford to further Edward's education, Walton making her thinking explicit. "She continued there with him, and still kept him in a moderate awe of herself, and so much under her own eye as to see and converse with him daily; but she managed this power over him without any such rigid sourness as might make her company a torment to her child, but with such a sweetness and compliance with the recreations and pleasures of youth, as did incline him willingly to spend much of his time in the company of his dear and careful mother; which was to her great content" (Lee, 175). A modern scholar has inferred, no doubt correctly, that "she had not much confidence in the morals of undergraduates."[6] Rossi has suggested that "the death of Richard, the marriage of her eldest son were for her a liberation; now she had a good excuse to leave the country and see the world."[7] Rossi's assertion is difficult to evaluate, as is his claim that the young husband had recourse to his studies as a refuge, "a world of his own" that allowed him to escape from a premature unwelcome marriage and a bossy interfering mother.[8]

London and Montgomery: 1600–1608. Herbert spent the years 1600–08 in London and Montgomery. He recalls meeting Queen Elizabeth at court, who inquired after the name of the handsome young fellow kneeling before her. Informed "who I was, and that

I had married Sir William Herbert of St. Julian's daughter," Herbert writes, "the Queen hereupon looked attentively upon me, and swearing her ordinary oath, said it is pity he was married so young" (Lee, 44). Herbert came of age in 1603 and promptly began to receive titles and offices. He was made a Knight of the Order of the Bath (1603), served in Parliament, and was appointed sheriff of Montgomery county (1605).

When in London, Herbert benefited from his mother's celebrated hospitality. Mingling with the scholars she took delight in entertaining, Herbert could have discussed poetry with John Donne, music (Herbert, like his brother George, was an accomplished lutenist) with William Byrd, history with William Camden.[9] Herbert would also have met a contemporary of his: another handsome young aristocrat, Sir John Danvers, who in 1609 would marry Herbert's mother. Donne's funeral sermon for Magdalen Herbert (in 1627) would argue that the young man and the woman twice his age blended together like the "higher and lower strings of one sound" into an "evenness" of years (Lee, 178). But from his failure to mention Danvers in his autobiography, it has been inferred that Herbert was not pleased with his mother's remarriage.[10]

Travels and Duels: 1608–1619

A citizen of the world. So far there are only a few points in Herbert's life story that in retrospect seem to prepare him for the work in philosophy of religion on which his fame rests. Heir to a distinguished family, he had the inclination to trust no judgment more than his own and the independence to pursue his thinking wherever it led him. (Being a lord can facilitate a man's philosophizing; consider Bacon or Russell.) Trained at Oxford to perform scholastic disputation in the ancient tongues, Herbert was equipped to read and write in Latin, the universal language of learning in the seventeenth century. But all students of Herbert's career agree that a prime factor behind his work was his experience abroad, especially in France. There he was exposed to a new realm of thought and conduct—to new varieties of religious passion and persecution, and to new forms of religious indifference.

Herbert had already learned French, Italian, and Spanish "without any master or teacher . . . by the help of some books in Latin or

English translated into those" languages and by the help of some dictionaries. "My intention in learning languages," Herbert proclaims ringingly, was "to make myself a citizen of the world as far as it were possible" (Lee, 23). The phrase calls up the image of the Stoic wise man, at home anywhere beneath the sky; and it looks forward to the universalism that Herbert will use as a polemical sword to cut through any particularity of creed. Finally, the phrase reminds us that Herbert was a young Elizabethan-become-Jacobean, ready to set out on a grand tour.

Quo vadis? Arriving in France in 1608 for the first of many visits, Herbert found a country at peace under Henry IV after a generation of civil war (1562–94) between Catholics and Protestants. France was now a magnet for young Englishmen of fashion. They came to master the courtly arts—riding, fencing, dancing, music-making in the proper French style.[11] For such were the studies of young French aristocrats, who were not packed off to university, but trained at academies in riding and fighting. French scholars of the day deplored the disesteem for letters and learning among the aristocracy, attributing it to the malign influence of the protracted civil wars.[12]

Herbert was befriended by an old soldier who was also one of the most distinguished noblemen of France, the duke of Montmorency. Though barely able to read, the duke had superb stables and an excellent riding master. Herbert devotes many pages of the autobiography to this "brave Constable" of France, though only a sentence to "that incomparable scholar Isaac Casaubon, by whose learned conversation I much benefited myself" (Lee, 56).

English moralists of the period were fond of railing against the ill effects of sending impressionable heirs to the wicked Latin countries of Western Europe. In 1617 Joseph Hall (later a bishop) published *Quo vadis? a just censure of travell as it is commonly undertaken by gentlemen of our nation.* He discussed the sad fate of "those, that profess to seek the glory of a perfect breeding, and the perfection of that, which we call Civility, in Travel: of which sort I have (not without indignation) seen too many lose their hopes, and themselves in the way; returning as empty of grace, and other virtues, as full of words, vanity, mis-dispositions." They bring home with them "that devilish art and practice of duel, wherein men seek honor in blood, and are taught the ambition of being glorious butchers of men." They also bring "that close Atheism, which secretly laughs God in the face, and thinks it weakness to believe, wisdom to profess any religion."[13]

Now Herbert's autobiography is full of duels and challenges, and he would soon be composing a powerfully critical book on religion, destined to earn him many accusations of secret atheism. So in his case Hall's charges would seem in some measure substantiated. Accordingly, it is worth looking at the French scene Herbert encountered through eyes less biased than those of the xenophobic future bishop.

The early decades of the seventeenth century in France were marked by what a modern historian calls a widely "diffused incredulity."[14] Much evidence supports the comment of a Frenchman of the day that "our wars for religion have made us forget religion."[15] Another Frenchman deplored "the paucity of religion that is evident in our nobles today." And a contemporary remarked that many persons "made it a point of pride to have no religion, as if their impiety could serve as a token of their courage."[16] In short, irreligion was fashionable, as another author argued in a book appropriately called *De la mode.*[17]

Herbert must have learned something of this current of thought from the Montmorency family. Among them, as Rossi notes, he would have heard jesting about the Church.[18] For a generation the Montmorencys had been a leading family of the French political group called the Politiques, which supported toleration for Protestants as a means of maintaining national peace and prosperity. The antitolerationist party saw in the Politique position an abandonment of religious conviction for political expediency—hence the name. Without a doubt, the Politiques drew to their ranks many liberal thinkers of the day.

The point of honor.   The great plague of dueling raged as never before or since at the time Herbert visited France. One contemporary witness reports that in the three years prior to 1609, nearly 2,500 French nobles lost their lives in duels. Venetian observers were shocked to note of the French aristocrats that "the greatest bond between them is that of the duel"; they "dare to fight for the flimsiest of reasons."[19] Contemporary sources tell of duels provoked by one gentleman's shadow interfering with that of another gentleman.[20] It is little wonder that Sir George Carew, English ambassador to France, reported in 1609 that he was "still much troubled here about the quarrels of the young gentlemen of our nation."[21] They were evidently playing up to the role of fighting-cock aristocrats that they saw around them.

What significance ought one to attribute to the duel? This question is a vital one for students of Herbert's life and works. An early seventeenth-century French writer explains "this miserable disorder of duels." "Everyone knows that this violence is produced by the liberty which so long, and so woeful civil wars . . . have brought."[22] George Carew thought that King Henry allowed duels to take place "to divide the nobles and to get rid of 'hot heads.' " King Henry himself argued that "the point of honor is dear and precious to the nobility, which prefers it to the preservation of its life, so that there is no hope that rigor or punishment will hold it in check or keep it from debating with arms."[23]

Supporters of the dueling system reminded contemporaries that the aim of a duel was "the revelation of the truth."[24] In his *Book of honor and arms* (1590), Sir William Segar explains that duels presuppose that God, who alone "know[s] the secret thoughts of all men . . . would give victory to him that justly adventured his life, for truth, honor, and justice."[25] The point was, of course, contested. In his *Institution of a Young Noble Man* (1607), James Cleland writes that he would not "have men think that God's assistance and power is ever tied unto their just cause; they tempt God in urging him every hour to work miracles, for justifying of their innocency, and condemning of the other's guiltiness."[26]

But dueling must be considered in the context of a system in which the struggle for precedence was never-ending. Everyone defended his smallest prerogatives with a fierce care almost unimaginable today. The theory of such behavior in its social context has been developed by Norbert Elias in his book *The Court Society*. Elias notes that while in the twentieth century "we like to objectify or reify everything personal, court people personify the objective." And "in such a society, the chance of preceding another, or sitting while he had to stand . . . were not mere externals. . . . They were literal documentations of social existence, notations of the place one currently occupied." Rising or falling in this court hierarchy "meant as much to the courtier as profit or loss to a businessman." Everything counts in such a society, for "behavior at any time and every day could decide a person's place."[27]

So when one finds Herbert in the autobiography repeatedly picking a quarrel over a ribbon plucked from a young woman's outfit, one should not speak, with Rossi, of Herbert's "obsession" with ribbons.[28] Instead one should recall Elias's account of what the French writer La Bruyère called the "serious, melancholy game" of life at court. It was a game at which Herbert was trying his hand during these years—at once lightheartedly and seriously. Herbert's awareness of the game is evident in the autobiography, as will be shown in the chapter devoted to that book. For now it suffices to bear in mind Elias's comment that "the art of what, with a characteristic narrowing of meaning, we call 'diplomacy' is . . . cultivated in the everyday life" at court.[29]

 Soldier and lover. During these years, Herbert did not spend all his time in France. He was often in England, where his exploits were of an amatory nature. After seeing his portrait, various ladies of fashion fell in love with him. And there was the occasional jealous husband to fight with. In 1611 one self-proclaimed cuckold (Herbert denied the charge) took four men with him to ambush Herbert "in a place called Scotland Yard." The passage in the autobiography describing the fight is far too long to quote, but it offers swashbuckling of a high order. Particularly charming is this sentence: "The dagger now sticking in me, Sir Henry Cary, afterwards Lord Falkland and Lord Deputy of Ireland, finding the dagger thus in my body, snatched it out." With insouciant wit, Herbert leaves the dagger (and the reader) dangling to identify the nobleman who came to his assistance. Outnumbered as he is, Herbert of course wins the battle. "I remained master of the place and his weapons." The aggressor is reported to have fled "vomiting all the way." This is comedy at its most high-spirited, the wounds seeming as unreal as those in a cartoon. Herbert later sends a message to the would-be assassin. "I desired to see him with his sword in his hand; the answer that he sent was, that I had whored his wife, and that he would kill me with a musket out of a window." And the comedy of the entire passage is heightened by the witty introduction in which Herbert denies that anything much

more than common civility ever passed betwixt us, though I confess I think no man was welcomer to her when I came, for which I shall allege this passage: Coming one day into her chamber, I saw her through the curtains lying upon her bed with a wax candle in one hand, and the picture I formerly mentioned [of Herbert] in the other. I coming thereupon

somewhat boldly to her, she blew out the candle, and hid the picture
from me; myself thereupon being curious to know what that was she held
in her hand, got the candle to be lighted again, by means whereof I found
it was my picture she looked upon with more earnestness and passion than
I could have easily believed, especially since myself was not engaged in
any affection towards her. (Lee, 69–73)

In these years Herbert also had some military experience. He
served as a gentleman volunteer with the Protestant forces during
the skirmishing in the Low Countries in 1610. The bone of contention between the Protestant and Catholic powers was the succession to the duchy of Cleves. In 1614 Herbert went again to the
Low Countries as the same dispute revived. After a warm welcome
from the Protestant Army, in which at least one of his brothers was
serving,[30] Herbert passed on through Germany to Italy.

Visiting the English Catholic College at Rome, he explained his
eagerness "to see the antiquities of the place; if without scandal to
the religion in which I was born and bred up, I may take this
liberty" (Lee, 83). As usual, Herbert's language here is notably
careful: he presents his adherence to Protestantism as a matter of
upbringing, not of belief. The hackneyed phrase "born and bred"
takes on an ironic force, if the reader of the autobiography knows
Herbert's views. Otherwise, the point will be missed and the reader
will deem him a conventional Protestant. Herbert goes on in the
autobiography to record his judgment that Rome was "that place,
which first found means to establish so great an empire over the
persons of men, and afterwards over their consciences, the articles
of confession and absolving sinners being a greater *arcanum imperii*
[secret of state] for governing the world, than all the arts invented
by statists [politicians] ever were" (Lee, 83). As this passage suggests, Herbert's hostility to Rome was not doctrinal but political.
Though neither a Protestant nor even a Christian, Herbert, like
many of his countrymen, was fervently opposed to the papacy and
to its close ally, the Spanish Crown. So Herbert could spend years
fighting for, pursuing diplomacy in behalf of, the Protestant cause
without himself believing in Protestant doctrine.

Returning from Italy in 1615, Herbert undertook to assist the
duke of Savoy in raising French Protestant troops to fight in the
duke's war against Spain. Arriving in Lyons, Herbert was promptly
arrested, the levying of such troops having been banned. An English

friend procured Herbert's release, and he went once again to the
Low Countries. He returned to London in 1616, a year in which
he suffered from what may have been malaria. Typically, Rossi
suggests that this recurrent disease may have served to provoke
Herbert's meditations on religion.[31]

The Ambassadorial Years

In 1619 Edward Herbert was appointed British ambassador to
Paris. This was probably "the most important post" the British had
to fill abroad,[32] and Rossi suggests that Herbert was chosen precisely
for his obscurity, with no serious regard for his qualifications.[33] But
even Rossi admits that none of the diplomatic correspondence—
often written by masters of gossip and character assassination—
questions Herbert's selection or shows any doubt of his competence
for the job. It was standard practice throughout Europe in that
period that most ambassadors' "training for diplomacy only began
with their actual service."[34]

In the autobiography, Herbert jests at the unexpectedness of his
appointment. When the Privy Council sent for him, he feared that
he was being called on the carpet for "some complaint, though false
. . . made against me" (Lee, 99). In Paris, Herbert soon showed
himself an adept diplomat, as Rossi himself allows.[35] Herbert quickly
assumed a leading role among diplomats in Paris working for international Protestantism and against Hapsburg Spain. A Venetian
diplomat refers to him as a fanatical Protestant.[36] Herbert took it
upon himself to work on behalf of the French Protestant Huguenots,
victims of renewed governmental persecution. And Herbert identified himself in particular with the Protestant side in the principal
dispute in Europe of 1619, that over Bohemia. (This was in fact
the opening round of the Thirty Years War.) When the Bohemians
revolted in 1618 against the Hapsburg emperor, they offered their
kingship to the Protestant Frederick, Elector Palatine, who was
King James's son-in-law. The Armies of the Catholic League defeated Frederick's forces at the Battle of the White Mountain in late
1620, and the ousted Frederick fled to plead for help from other
Protestant rulers.

But this is to get ahead of the story. In 1619, the English viewed
the offer of the Bohemian crown to Frederick as, quite literally, a
godsend. Protestant theorists of history saw in Frederick's oppor-

tunity the beginning of "the final struggle between the godly and the papal Antichrist."[37] The fulfillment of all the prophecies of the Book of Revelation was at hand. And while Herbert avoids the specifically biblical scenario, he shares his countrymen's enthusiasm. In a dispatch to London of September 1619, Herbert notes that a question has been raised "whether the Palatine will accept the offer. But God forbid he should refuse it, being the apparent way His providence has opened to the ruin of the Papacy. I hope therefore his Majesty will assist in this great work."[38]

To the world's astonishment, however, King James watched as his daughter and son-in-law were defeated and driven into exile. Herbert's anguish over their fate is clear in his diplomatic papers. Reprimanded for doing too much for the Elector, his requests for detailed instructions from London ignored,[39] Herbert professed himself "so limited in this affair of Bohemia that I can only pray the earnest providence to turn all to the best."[40] French courtiers mocked Herbert's efforts to attain French neutrality in the war. If the Elector's cause were any good, they argued plausibly, his father-in-law would be supporting him publicly.

James refused to budge, "being that pacific prince all the world knew," as Herbert puts it with a touch of mockery (Lee, 113). Nor was Herbert the only Jacobean diplomat kept in the dark as to his master's intentions. Such ignorance was in fact a central structural feature of James's foreign policy. He had two foreign secretaries, each reporting to him separately, each corresponding with a different group of English diplomats. One dealt with those diplomats (including Herbert) who worked against the interests of the Hapsburg powers; the other set worked in favor of those interests. Only James had all the cards in his hand. And only he knew "the anti-Spanish program was only a counterpoint, not the main theme."[41] James was following Queen Elizabeth's policy of avoiding major military involvement on the Continent. And what Rossi (in line with the traditional view that goes back to the early seventeenth century) condemns as shortsighted, cowardly behavior, more recent historians have begun to commend. Conrad Russell writes that "on foreign affairs and religion, James should be given credit for a considerable measure of success." Like his predecessor, "he kept his intentions obscure, even to his own ministers. Whatever is regarded as successful and prudent policy in one ruler should be so regarded in another."[42]

Balancing overtures to Spain with approaches to France, James played a game of three-handed duplicity in which no two-party deal could long endure, each party to it quickly competing to betray its new partner with the excluded third power. And when James's negotiations to marry the Prince of Wales to a Spanish princess—negotiations Herbert had opposed on strong grounds—failed, the turn came for a French princess. And at this point the French maneuvered to get Herbert out of office. He would be too little inclined to make concessions, as Rossi puts it.[43] So in 1624 his diplomatic career came to an end.

What Herbert learned in these years was vital. He had ample opportunity to observe "the manner wherein the French are now grown such masters that they do all their business in compliment, the outward sense and meaning being only the cipher and dead letter of their intentions."[44] As an ambassador, Herbert had been obliged to adopt some of that same manner himself. After all, according to the definition of a fellow British diplomat of the day, "a resident ambassador is a man sent to tell lies abroad for his country's good."[45] Even Renaissance books on the perfect ambassador stated that he was above all an orator.[46] And an orator makes the best case for whatever position he finds himself obliged to present. (Today the closest analogue is the trial lawyer.) And throughout the autobiography and the diplomatic dispatches from Paris, one sees Herbert's great pride in his skill at making a case. He delights in nothing more than in coming up with a witty argument that leaves the other side at a loss. Such an argument does "not satisfy" but "at least silences" the opposing debater.[47] Herbert's other resource as a diplomatic orator was indirection. Explaining in one of his dispatches how he made a particular point, he writes, "Though I speak not directly, I yet often convey and insinuate into their ears."[48]

The diplomatic years also produced or intensified Herbert's aversion to priests—to Catholic ones, at any rate. His correspondence is full of acid references to "the bigot party" and "the seditious Priests and Jesuits."[49] Another notable point in the diplomatic papers is Herbert's appeal for a secular, as opposed to a particular religious, way of looking at foreign affairs. Herbert urged the French to reject what he called the Jesuit claim that religion was the primary factor in the Bohemian war. "I . . . often told them that [that] reason would divide Christendom; for though the affair of Bohemia was not every man's quarrel, Religion was."[50] Of course, in saying this Herbert is following James's line that the Bohemian war was not a religious dispute, a line intended to keep Catholic powers like Spain from intervening. As happens so often, though, what seems like a commonplace takes on new meaning when spoken by a deist. For Herbert, clearly, religion was the stuff of quarrels.

Authorship. Before his return to England in the summer of 1624, Herbert arranged in Paris for the publication of his first book, *De Veritate,* in a small private edition not intended for sale. In the concluding pages of the autobiography as we have it, Herbert records that, after two leading Protestant theologues (Tilenus and Grotius) had urged him to publish, he was still hesitant. So he prayed for "some sign from heaven," without which he would "suppress" the book. "I had no sooner spoken these words, but a loud though yet gentle noise came from the heavens, for it was like nothing on earth, which did so comfort and cheer me, that I took my petition as granted, and that I had the sign I demanded, whereupon also I resolved to print my book" (Lee, 133–34). Rossi shows that this sign from heaven has to date from the summer of 1623.[51] But the authenticity of the event has been questioned. Some readers find in the passage a tone of utter sincerity; others read it as deadpan mockery. The point is best treated in the chapter on the autobiography.

Herbert's public career after 1624 is not a happy one. Sidney Lee, whose slighting of Herbert far exceeds Rossi's, calls the later years "a dreary series of disasters" (Lee, xxi). Heavily in debt from his ambassadorial outlays (the usual situation of a Renaissance diplomat), Herbert waited years for the honors that were in his view owed him for his service in Paris. He became a member of the King's Council of War in 1624. That same year he was admitted to the Irish peerage as Lord Herbert of Castle Island (county Kerry); this estate had been colonized by Herbert's father-in-law.[52] Herbert had to rest content with what Rossi calls "this paltry noble title"[53] until 1629, when he became an English baron, at last Lord Herbert of Cherbury, the name by which he is known to history.

Herbert's successes in the later years were literary. He continued his research and writing. Rossi notes that "Herbert desired to become known as a writer but had no preference for" any particular kind of writing, letting circumstances dictate the subject of his works.[54] This is very much to overstate the disparateness of Herbert's books. But certainly his volumes of history were undertaken to seek favor at court. Nothing else could account for Herbert's agreeing to work over the duke of Buckingham's notes defending his generalship on the 1627 expedition to the Isle of Rhé. After Buckingham's assassination, Herbert completed the work and presented it in 1630 to the king, one of the few Englishmen grieving over the death of the much hated royal favorite. Herbert's next historical project was undertaken at the king's behest: a full history of Charles's brilliant and dominating sixteenth-century predecessor, Henry VIII, an assignment on which Herbert labored from 1632 to 1639. As will be made clear in the chapter on Herbert as historian, winning favor from the court was by no means the only motive at work in these large books.

One episode from Herbert's literary career in the 1630s merits mention. Though *De Veritate* had been placed on the Catholic Church's Index of Forbidden Books in 1633, an Italian priest named Gregorio Panzani tried to sound out Herbert on his attitude toward Rome. Panzani had been sent to England (1634–36) to explore the possibilities for Catholicism in a court whose Queen was herself a Catholic. Historians agree that Panzani was "a vain and credulous man," whose "gullibility about English sympathy for Rome was boundless."[55] In 1635 Panzani reported to his superior that Herbert was "a very moderate man, well disposed toward Rome in particular, because a book of his entitled *De Veritate* has not been severely censured, of which fact he boasts." Herbert's characteristic deadpan has utterly gulled the Italian. A few months later, Panzani reported on further conversations with "Milord Herbert" in which "he many times professed to recognize the Roman Church as Mother of all the Churches."[56] Panzani gushed over the possibility of regaining England for the Roman fold. What Herbert must have meant, though, is something very different: as a later author put the deist view, "The name *Church* signifies only a self-interested Party."[57]

Herbert published new editions of *De Veritate* in 1633 and 1645, the latter together with two supplementary works: *De Causis Errorum (The Causes of Errors)* and *De Religio Laici (A Layman's Religion)*. In 1639 a French version of *De Veritate* was printed. Herbert's historical studies both appeared posthumously, the biography of Henry VIII in 1649 and the study of the expedition to Rhé in 1656. (The latter work, addressed to a European audience, came out in Latin; Herbert's original English text was not published until 1860.) Most of the books Herbert wrote in the last years before his death in 1648 appeared posthumously: *De Religione Gentilium (The Religion of the Gentiles)* in Amsterdam in 1663; the autobiography in 1764; and *A Dialogue between a Tutor and his Pupil,* Herbert's most daring presentation in English of his philosophy of religion, in 1768. In 1665 Henry Herbert had published his brother's English and Latin poems.

The Civil War. The Civil War years were difficult ones for Herbert. Uncommitted to either side in what came increasingly to be recognized as a religious dispute, Herbert attempted to sit on the fence. Such a stance provoked the distrust of both sides, who believed that (as the title of a contemporary pamphlet puts it) "neutrality is malignancy."[58] When his attempt to remain neutral proved impossible to maintain, Herbert showed himself to be what contemporaries called an "ambidexter," someone "prepared to adopt any political stance which would limit the hazards of war."[59]

At first Herbert supported King Charles, joining his monarch in the expedition against the Scots in 1639. In the House of Lords, Herbert spoke for moderation; on one occasion in 1642 he was taken into custody for a remark deemed too favorable to the king. Returning to Wales, Herbert pled infirmity when called upon to raise troops for the king. And he refused to accept a garrison of Royalist troops at Montgomery Castle. Herbert's reluctance stands out in this context: Wales was predominantly Royalist, and members of Herbert's family (including his brother Henry) served their king faithfully. Yet in September 1644, when parliamentary forces arrived at the gates of Montgomery Castle, a strategic spot in Wales, Herbert surrendered without a shot being fired.

Condemned by the Royalists as a traitor, Herbert would bear this obloquy for centuries. Sidney Lee asserts that "Lord Herbert saved his property at the expense of his honor" (Lee, xxiii). The Montgomeryshire historian who published the documents of Herbert's surrender paints a different picture: "the aged and sick nobleman, roused at midnight from his bed by a peremptory summons to surrender his castle to a besieging force which had gained possession of the outworks and was prepared to force an entrance, deserted by his terrorised servants, and thus apparently forced to surrender."[60] A recent historian of *The Royalist War Effort 1642–46* summarizes the taking of Montgomery Castle in this way: "This fortress, reputedly impregnable, had been one of the few left in the hands of its owner, Lord Herbert of Cherbury, who betrayed this trust by surrendering upon the first summons. He was escorted happily into retirement at London, out of the reach of the enraged Royalists, who included his son Richard."[61]

Herbert brought with him to London a certificate from the parliamentary commander Thomas Middleton to the effect that Herbert had long been well disposed toward Parliament, whatever appearances "might argue the contrary."[62] In London, Herbert persuaded the parliamentarians to reinstate him in possession of his goods, which had been sequestered on grounds of his supposed Royalist sympathies. From this point on Herbert was treated generously by the parliamentary side.

A philosophical death.   Herbert died in London during the first days of August 1648.[63] The manner of his death was of interest to many, as would be the case with later deist philosophers like Voltaire. Christian apologists argued that deists and atheists died in raging terror of the afterlife; deists insisted that their masters expired serenely, "philosophically." And Herbert, that "scandalously heretical lord" (as William Empson calls him),[64] provided a good test case.

Unbelievers in eighteenth-century France would make a high art of dying "like a philosopher." The key point, they would argue, was "to evade the clergy rather than defy them." To cause scandal by one's deathbed defiance could lead to denial of civilized burial and could cause other problems for one's heirs.[65] A century earlier, Herbert had shown how a deist philosopher ought to die.

John Aubrey, that sublime gossip, tells the story in his *Brief Lives*. "James Usher, Lord Primate of Ireland, was sent for by him, when in his death-bed, and he would have received the sacrament. He said indifferently of it that *if there was good in anything 'twas in that,* or *if it did no good 'twould do no hurt.* The Primate refused it, for which many blamed him. He then turned his head to the other side and expired very serenely."[66]

Ever the diplomat, Herbert asked to receive the sacrament, but in language of such patent ambiguity that the priest could not in conscience offer it. A learned and tolerant man, a good friend of Herbert's friend and executor, John Selden, Usher must have known what game Herbert was playing. He would have understood the view of deathbed conversions that Herbert shared with Selden. In John Selden's *Table-Talk,* one reads that "for a priest to turn a man when he lies a dying, is just like one that hath a long time solicited a woman, and cannot obtain his end; at length makes her drunk, and so lies with her."[67]

John Donne's poem "To Sir Edward Herbert, at Juliers" (1610) concludes with a discussion of the different effects knowledge can have on different people: "poisonous, or purgative, or cordial." Donne addresses Herbert:

> As brave as true, is that profession then
> Which you do use to make; that you know man.
> This makes it credible, you have dwelt upon
> All worthy books, and now are such a one.
> Actions are authors, and of those in you
> Your friends find every day a mart of new.[68]

Donne argues that, in Herbert's case, book and man are interchangeable: the man is a book ("you are one") and his actions can be read as texts expressive of character ("actions are authors"). This chapter has shown the correctness of Donne's assertion. Subsequent chapters will demonstrate that the converse is also true. Herbert's books are to be read as "actions" of the author whose character is revealed by such other actions as his manner of death.

Chapter Two
De Veritate and Deism

Herbert's tombstone identifies him (in Latin) as "Baron of Cherbury and Castle Island, author of the book whose title is *De Veritate*."[1] It is this work, first published in 1624, that has earned Lord Herbert his place in intellectual history.

Several editions of the Latin original appeared in the seventeenth century, the most authoritative being the one published at London in 1645. A French translation came out in 1639, but no English version existed until 1937. Even in Meyrick Carré's careful English rendering, *De Veritate* is not an easy book to read. Almost without exception, though, the difficulties of the English translation are those of Herbert's Latin original. Some readers may, in moments of exasperation, wish that Carré had ventured a more interpretive translation, abandoning literality in favor of clarity. But the reader who can compare the English with the Latin will recognize the extraordinary difficulty of the task Carré faced. The translator notes that "Herbert's style is notorious. . . . The Latin is tortuous and pedantic."[2]

Carré devotes some fifty pages of his introduction to a summary of the book's argument. Rossi's interpretive commentary is nearly as long as the work it treats, which runs precisely 250 pages in the 1645 edition. The present study cannot pretend to follow every turn in Herbert's argument with similar precision. Nor need it. The nature and import of *De Veritate* will stand out most clearly when it is viewed from a certain distance. Read as a proposed solution to a particular set of problems at a given moment in intellectual history, the book speaks clearly and powerfully. One need have no doubt of the thrust and purport of Herbert's first book, whatever the awkwardnesses or difficulties of this or that passage of scholastic argumentation.

Much of *De Veritate* is devoted to a critical account of epistemology—that is, theory of knowledge. Herbert considers the different ways in which humans have access to information about the world and themselves, and the varying reliability of these ways of knowing. In so doing, of course, Herbert comes up against every traditional problem in epistemology, and the historian of philosophy can have a field day citing sources and analogues across the tradition from Plato through Peirce. Looked at in this way, the book appears as "an eclectic string of incompatible doctrines drawn from a multitude of sources. In it the minced Aristotelianism of the university courses is thrown together with fragments of the anti-Aristotelianism of the previous age. The main doctrine of the work is derived from the Neo-Platonic current of sixteenth-century speculation."[3] The words are Carré's, but the view they present is one he shares with Rossi. In his first publication on Herbert, Rossi treats *De Veritate* as a "patchwork" of incompatible ideas about truth and knowledge. Rossi characterizes Herbert's procedure thus: "Instead of discarding any presupposition about the nature of truth he accepts all possible presuppositions and endeavors to reconcile them."[4]

Read in this fashion, Herbert's book is out of focus. For *De Veritate* was not intended to be a contribution to technical epistemology as practiced by academic philosophers, however much it apes their vocabulary. As Charles de Rémusat noted more than a century ago, at the root of *De Veritate* lies Herbert's concern with religious truth.[5] The point was quite clear to hostile theologues in the seventeenth and eighteenth centuries; accordingly, as citations later in this chapter will show, they are often better guides to Herbert's book than twentieth-century historians of philosophy. They had no doubt that (as Charles Lyttle asserted in a fine essay of 1935) "the author's central meaning . . . is essentially religious, and not epistemological at all." Lyttle calls the epistemological component of *De Veritate* an "imposing facade."[6] That formulation perhaps goes a bit too far. Preferable is the judicious statement of the most recent commentator on Herbert's philosophy, R. D. Bedford: *"De Veritate* has the air of being a necessary evil, a strenuous accumulation of abstract argument and demonstration, vital to the cause, necessary to the complete and respectable picture, but impelled by, and finally breaking out in, a strongly ethical and moral purpose."[7]

The present chapter offers a reading of *De Veritate* not primarily as a treatise on epistemology, but as a philosophical charter for the religious doctrine called natural religion or deism (both terms will be carefully defined below). Such is the role the work has played in intellectual history, and that was precisely what Herbert intended.

The Intellectual Context

Polemics and skepticism. Behind all Herbert's writing on religion lies the bitter awareness of continuing interfaith strife. The cold and hot warfare between Catholics and Protestants (and among Protestants of different stripes) was entering its second century. Some weary laymen began to wonder if confidence could be invested in any of the squabbling churches. And their doubt was heightened by the skillful marshaling of powerful new dialectical weapons.

The story has been expertly told by Richard Popkin in *The History of Scepticism from Erasmus to Descartes,* without question the best book in English on the intellectual context in which *De Veritate* was composed. Popkin explains how the doctrines of ancient skepticism, rediscovered in the sixteenth century, were brought to bear in the ongoing "dispute over the proper standard of religious knowledge, or what was called 'the rule of faith.' " To judge correctly among the competing claims of rival religious groups, one needed precisely such "a 'rule of faith,' a criterion for distinguishing true faith from false faith." But the dialecticians on each side had an easy time showing the weaknesses of their opponent's criterion. As a tool for undermining the foundations of any proffered claim to knowledge, skepticism became the prevailing technique of refutation.[8]

The danger, of course, lay in the symmetry of the disputes. The same skeptical arguments with which one devastated the other side were applied in return to one's own position. Soon Protestants and Catholics were accusing one another of being closet skeptics. The other side was thought to be sowing doubt in order to compel sheer surrender to its own authority.

To escape from the vicious reciprocity of this debate, some thinkers had recourse to a doctrine that has come to be known as fideism. This offers a means of employing the weapons of skepticism without oneself becoming vulnerable to their rebounding on one's own position. The fideist raises doubt as to the possibility of giving rational justification for any belief; but the fideist, removing the intellectual grounds of belief, leaves the way clear for a belief otherwise motivated. Of course, such blind faith may satisfy the individual; but the fideist position entirely abandons the quest for a criterion or rule of faith defensible on rational grounds.

Fideism could not resolve the overall "skeptical crisis" that was the dominant fact of intellectual affairs in the seventeenth century.

A "quest for certainty" to resolve this crisis underlies much of the philosophical activity of the period.

Toleration. If the quest for certainty is the theoretical reflection of the crisis of the period, then the movement for reconciliation and toleration is the practical reflection of that crisis. Throughout the period of religious strife, there were men and women who claimed that none of the points at issue among the competing churches were fundamental to religious life or to individual salvation. A French ambassador to England in 1597 reported that Queen Elizabeth "told [him] that if there were two Princes in Christendom who had good will and courage it would be easy to reconcile the differences in religion; for there was only one Jesus Christ and one faith, and all the rest that they disputed about but trifles."[9]

Such irenic or conciliatory sentiments met countervailing pressures in Renaissance England. Christian disunity was, all agreed, a manifest scandal. But the Reformation had created an immense distrust of Roman Catholics among the Protestant faithful. For them, as Conrad Russell writes, "it was not a point of conscience to resist prejudice, but to indulge it." For "if all differences [in belief] were fundamental, Protestants were led to consider [Catholics], not as misguided Christians, but as akin to infidels."[10]

Nonetheless, historians of the idea of toleration have shown the gradual emergence in England of the view that all Christians (of any, or no, denomination) share a common, soul-saving faith. These currents of thought have been traced in the multivolume histories by W. K. Jordan (for England) and Joseph Lecler (for all of Europe)—works of scholarship highly recommended to the general reader. Here there is space to point to one early figure: Jacobus Acontius, an Italian Catholic who became a naturalized Protestant Englishman. His Latin treatise *Satan's Stratagems* (1565) offers the earliest systematic case for toleration. The psychological penetration is acute as Acontius shows Satan at work promoting not heresy, but persecution. Acontius held the view (in Jordan's words) "that there was much truth in all of the Christian systems and likewise much that was either wrong or unessential in them." He called for agreement on the few fundamentals requisite for salvation in order to " 'suppress much of the cackle of men' and . . . eliminate many of the scandals which impede the course of the Church."[11]

A similar view was held two generations later by Hugo Grotius, one of the scholars to whom Herbert had shown the manuscript of

De Veritate. A refugee to France from Holland, where his irenic sympathies in religion had helped win him a lifetime sentence of imprisonment, Grotius in 1622 wrote a treatise entitled *De Veritate Religionis Christianae.*[12] Intended in the first instance for missionaries, Grotius's book propounded a generalized Christianity not to be identified with that of any particular sect. Grotius stressed ethical over dogmatic issues. He hoped to ground religion upon reciprocal tolerance and general agreement on a few clear beliefs common to all. He wrote, "The difference of opinions that is amongst Christians doth not hinder the common consent and agreement in those fundamental principles, for which chiefly we have commended Christian Religion."[13]

In many respects Grotius's *De Veritate Religionis Christianae* runs parallel with Herbert's *De Veritate.* But the qualifying genitive phrase that extends Grotius's title points up the difference between the two thinkers. As Mario Sina writes: "The requirements of rational clarity, of moral purity, of fraternity and concord were absorbed by Herbert of Cherbury [from Grotius]. The same necessity, that of arriving at a clear and definitive formulation of the essential points of true religion, animates the pages of this work of Grotius and those of Herbert's *De Veritate* dedicated to the formulation of the 'common notions about religion.' With a single, but fundamental difference: while the work of Grotius (and those of the liberal theologians in general) was a defense of Christianity, the work of Herbert was a defense of natural religion." While Grotius exalted Christianity above any other religion, Herbert distinguished between all particular religions (including Christianity) and (in Sina's phrase) "the one true and sublime religion, that of nature."[14] In short, Grotius was a tolerant Christian; Herbert was a deist.

Deism

Deism represented another response to the "skeptical crisis." Where fideism abandoned rational tests of faith, deism proclaimed only the rationally apprehensible to be worthy of faith.

Before discussing the emergence of deism in the two generations before *De Veritate,* it is essential to clear up a possible misunderstanding. Words have histories of their own, and that of *deism* is notably intricate. In the eighteenth century the term came to refer to a particular relationship presumed to obtain between God and the world. Like a watchmaker, the Creator was said to have left his creation to run according to its own inner workings. The doctrine of an absentee God was called philosophical deism. This later sense of the term must be distinguished from the meaning it bore in the sixteenth and seventeenth centuries. [15]

Deism is based on *deus* (the Latin for "God"), no doubt on the analogy of *atheism* (from *theos,* the equivalent Greek word). The original sense of *deism* is well conveyed by the first recorded use of the word, a French passage many times reprinted by scholars since the time Pierre Bayle included it in his famous *Historical and Critical Dictionary.* The author is the French Calvinist theologian Pierre Viret; in a preface to his *Instruction Chrestienne* (1564), Viret warns against the menace of a new variety of unbelief:

There are several who indeed profess to believe that there is some Deity or God, as the Turks and Jews do: but as for Jesus Christ, and all those things which the doctrine of the Evangelists and Apostles testifies concerning him, they take them for fables and dreams. . . . I hear that some of this band call themselves Deists, a new word in opposition to that of Atheists. For the word Atheist signifies one that is without God, so they would hereby signify, that they are not without God, because they believe that there is one . . . but as for Jesus Christ, they do not know who he is. . . . [T]hey accommodate themselves to the religion of those with whom they are obliged to live, out of complaisance or fear. . . . I am struck with horror, when I think that there are such monsters among those who bear the name of Christians. [16]

In 1628 a French historian named Scipion du Pleix defined deists as "those who indeed believe that there is an eternal divinity . . . who governs the world, but who cannot savor the mysteries of the Christian religion." [17] Preaching in Northampton, Massachusetts, in 1739, Jonathan Edwards noted that "the Deists wholly cast off the Christian religion. . . . Indeed they own the being of God; but deny that Christ was the Son of God, and say he was a mere cheat; and so they say all the prophets and apostles were; and they deny the whole Scripture. They deny that any of it is the word of God. They deny any revealed religion . . . and say that God has given mankind no other light to walk by but their own reason." [18]

Many commentators on deism in the seventeenth century were certain that deism was really (in the words of the French bishop Bossuet) "a disguised atheism." [19] In his Boyle Lectures on *The Folly of Atheism* (1692), Richard Bentley condemned "some infidels among us" who "to avoid the odious name of *Atheists,* would shelter and screen themselves under a new one of *Deists,* which is not quite so obnoxious."[20]

Renaissance polemicists had a very wide notion of atheism. As D. C. Allen explains, "an atheist was one who could not accept any religious principles shared by all Christian creeds. A Jew, a Mohammedan, a deist was an atheist."[21] And some deists may in fact have been atheists in the twentieth-century sense of the word—unbelievers in any deity whatever. But there is little reason to doubt the sincerity with which most deists professed their belief in a Supreme Being, whom they chose to worship in accordance with what was called natural religion.

Deists distinguished between the various positive (from the Latin, the word means "arbitrarily laid down") religions—such as Judaism, Christianity, and the like—and the supposedly unique natural religion. Of the latter George Sabine has given an admirably clear definition:

In substance the doctrine meant that some religious beliefs—particularly in the existence of God, the immortality of the soul, and moral responsibility—are so manifest to human reason that they are natural to all men, that these beliefs form the significant core of all positive religions, except in so far as the latter have become irrational and corrupt, and that accordingly they include all that is needed for a religious life in this world and for salvation in the world to come. Obviously such a view tended to minimize . . . revelation, dogma, miracle, ritualistic observance, ecclesiastical organization, and the supposedly unique truth of Christianity or any other positive religion.[22]

Christian theologians generally included elements of natural religion in their apologetic systems as a first argument against atheism in the strict sense of the term. But for the Christian, natural religion remains a stepping-stone to revelation. "What distinguished the deist," as Roland Stromberg points out, "was not an interest in natural religion, but the belief that natural religion *alone* was sufficient, without need for any Christian revelation."[23] As a late seventeenth-century English writer put it, deism "is a denial of all revealed religion."[24]

Much of the early history of the deist movement is conjectural. The first notices come from the pens of hostile witnesses like Viret.

Nor is that fact surprising. It must be borne in mind that during the sixteenth century mere possession of a heretical book could be dangerous—let alone authorship and publication of such a work. In England, "openly expressed disbelief in Christianity carried heavy penalities, in theory the severest until the later seventeenth century."[25] Consequently, deism was at first transmitted by oral instruction. There are exceptions, like the booklet entitled *La Béatitude des Chrestiens* that Geoffroy Vallée published in 1573. This indubitably deist work earned its author death by burning in the following year. Other sixteenth-century writings propounded deism, but they remained unpublished until the nineteenth century.[26]

As early as 1754, John Leland gave an accurate statement of the early history of deism. (Indeed, Leland's *A View of the Principal Deistical Writers* remains a model of fair and judicious scholarship on the subject—remarkably so, since Leland was no friend of deism.) Leland writes, "The name of Deists, as applied to those who are no friends to revealed religion, is said to have been first assumed about the middle of the sixteenth century, by some gentlemen in France and Italy, who were willing to cover their opposition to the Christian revelation by a more honorable name than that of Atheists." Leland was well aware of the fact that the early deists could not speak freely. Hence, as he notes, their "attempts to subvert [Christianity's] divine authority" were "carried on sometimes under various disguises, and at other times [Leland must mean his own century] without any disguise at all."[27]

In the case of Herbert, Leland cites some passages that seem to suggest a favorable disposition on Herbert's part toward Christianity. The overall tendency of the writings, however, points unmistakably the other way. Leland writes:

I am sorry that I am obliged to say, that notwithstanding these fair professions, his Lordship on all occasions insinuateth prejudices against all revealed religion, as absolutely uncertain, and of little or no use. He inveigheth promiscuously, as many others have done since, against all pretenses to revelation, without making a distinction between the false and the true. He often speaks to the disadvantage of *particular religion,* which is a name he bestoweth upon the Christian religion. . . . And he representeth it as containing doctrines, which disgust some men against all religion, and therefore is for recommending what he calls the universal religion, as the best way to prevent men's having no religion at all.[28]

As an introduction to Herbert's *De Veritate,* this passage from Leland could hardly be bettered.

The Argument of *De Veritate*

Authority and consent.   In the preface to *De Veritate* Herbert asserts, "The work is published with the aim not of arousing controversy, but of closing it, or at any rate, making it unnecessary" (74). The chaos of disagreement around him is overwhelming, as Herbert makes evident on the opening page of the book: "The multitude of sects, divisions, sub-divisions and cross-divisions in the schools hopelessly distract the wits of the learned and the consciences of the unlettered." Intellectual alienation has gone so far that transmitted texts have become obstacles to real thinking: "The conclusions arrived at in former ages have now come to weigh so heavily upon our own reflections, that there is scarcely anyone in the world who is content to pursue an independent path in the search for truth; every one submits himself to some alien Church or School; thereby wholly renouncing his own powers" (75).

Some of these "sects," "as if to reap advantage" from the prevailing "dissension," have put forward "a strange and unprecedented philosophy . . . which superseded reason altogether and sought to establish its doctrines upon the basis of an implicit faith; inclining, indeed, thereby to that school which taught that it was impossible to know anything." This fideistic doctrine Herbert deems unacceptable: "Those who prefer faith to reason pass judgment on the facts before the case is argued." Moreover, the claim that reason must yield to faith could be presented on behalf of any faith, however spurious: "Is there, in a word, any imposture for which this way of arguing would not be free to plead?" (76–77).

Nevertheless, Herbert writes, "some spirit of truth pervades this shapeless and monstrous chaos of beliefs, informing its very errors with life and motion; and it is this spirit that I propose . . . to examine, to clarify and to defend" (75). In pursuit of that spirit Herbert abandons authority—both the authority of the sects and the authority of transmitted texts. "I cast aside these books, and addressed myself to the construction of my own ideas of truth" (78). Not that his findings are in any way idiosyncratic. "I am far from seeking to establish any new theory. On the contrary my conclusions are those which have been most widely accepted by every type of philosophy, religion and period" (81).

Man cannot know everything, Herbert admits, "but I think there are some things which can be known. And they are those which are testified to by the presence of a faculty, though the faculty and the object are not necessarily in conformity with each other even when they are both present" (78). Here some of Herbert's special vocabulary emerges. A faculty is a power of the soul through which objects are known—objects in the broadest sense of the term, including objects of thought. Truth is "a conformity between objects and faculties" (78). And "every object corresponds to a reciprocal faculty in us" (91).

At this point an oddity of usage becomes evident. Herbert holds that "every new object enters into conformity with a new faculty" (110). That means that the number of faculties in one individual is "unlimited" (113). A seventeenth-century commentator hostile to Herbert's deism wrote mockingly, "I am not willing to think that I have as many different faculties as there are different plants in my garden, or books in my study, or sentences in those books."[29] For purposes of exposition, though, one must accept the oddity of usage and try to see what end it serves in Herbert's system. No small point is at stake. Herbert will soon be writing: "Look into your own faculties and you will find God, virtue, and universal eternal truths" (121).

The essential point for Herbert is the providentially preestablished harmony between objects and faculties. "Whatever is true . . . is readily believed, because . . . objects correspond harmoniously with faculties, and faculties with objects" (80). A good way to get at Herbert's meaning is to recall the etymology of the word: *faculty* (Latin *facultas*) is from the Latin root that gives us the English words *facile* and *facility*. And for Herbert, a faculty is a power of the soul that (if intervening conditions are right) works easily, instantaneously, as if by itself. An English philosopher of the later seventeenth century named Richard Burthogge accurately captured Herbert's doctrine in this paraphrase: "Truth is so domestical and congruous to the faculty, so analogous and fit to it, that the inclination of the mind thereto, in nature and necessity, resembles that of a stone . . . to the center" of the earth.[30]

Accordingly, to learn the truth about the world, one need only examine one's own faculties, which (by definition in Herbert's system) correspond to every component of reality. This is true not only of simple perception—as of animals or plants—but also of religious and ethical intuition. Herbert writes, "So when we are bidden to give thanks to God, or to pursue justice, or courage, or temperance, an inner assent . . . is given, and an inner faculty replies and teaches us that the matter is actually what we perceive it to be" (81). One might object that different persons could have different notions of what justice means. But Herbert has an answer ready.

Herbert takes it to be the case that "the same faculties have been imprinted on the soul of every normal person in all ages" (78–79). If all individuals possess the same faculties, and if these faculties correspond to reality, then one has available a simple test of truth. "Whatever is believed by universal consent must be true and must have been brought into conformity in virtue of some internal faculty." Indeed, "universal consent . . . will be found to be the final test of truth" (116–17).

By this point in the exposition, it is emerging that Herbert has designed his epistemology as a weapon with which to defend his deist religion. Just how the defense works will become clear in the following discussion of what might be called Herbert's psychology: his treatment of the classes of faculties that account for the different classes of knowledge men possess. In those chapters, as at every point in *De Veritate,* the reader must bear in mind that overt epistemology or psychology is, in fact, covert religious polemic. To evade institutional pressures, Herbert abandons history: he maneuvers the reader into seeking what must be true given the nature of the human mind. "Let everyone," he writes, "retire into himself and refer all the theories of the authorities to his own faculties" (241).

The classes of knowledge. Herbert distinguishes four classes of faculties: natural instinct, internal apprehension, external apprehension, and discursive thought (115). Internal apprehension is roughly equivalent to the emotions, and external apprehension means sense perception; neither of these requires comment here. The heart of Herbert's polemically motivated psychology of knowledge lies in the relation between natural instinct and discursive thought.

Natural instinct is closely linked—at points virtually identified—with what Herbert calls Common Notions: "principles which it is not legitimate to dispute; they form that part of knowledge with which we were endowed in the primeval plan of Nature" (121). Herbert writes that "the Creator himself is revealed in some of these Common Notions" (126). As Rossi puts it, the Common Notions make up a "permanent revelation"[31] that is "imprinted" (to cite Herbert's favorite image) "on the soul by the dictates of nature itself" (106).

Herbert adds a proviso. He does not "call these notions common because they are revealed in every man, whether he will or no; they are termed common because they would be so but for the fact that we ourselves prevent them entering our minds" (126–27). Nonetheless, the Common Notions form the basis of that "Universal Consent," which (Herbert insists) "must be taken to be the beginning and end of theology and philosophy" (118).

The Common Notions suggest—as historians of philosophy never fail to note—a certain foreshadowing of elements of Kantian philosophy in that they are constitutive of, and not derived from, experience. Herbert is appealingly clear on this point. "The Common Notions must be deemed not so much the outcome of experience as principles without which we should have no experience at all" (132; cf. 105).

The Common Notions have as their ultimate goal "the preservation of individuals, species, general classes and the Universe itself" (135). Herbert contends, "In treating of these Notions I am defending God's cause, Who has bestowed Common Notions upon all men in all ages as media of his divine universal Providence" (118).

These Common Notions work through Natural Instinct, defined by Herbert (with his characteristic blithe circularity) as "the faculty which conforms with Common Notions" (116). The word *instinct* may seem surprising, but it precisely conveys Herbert's meaning with its suggestion of inborn, automatic response. As Herbert says, "It is the nature of natural instinct to fulfill itself irrationally, that is to say without foresight" (120). Like the animals, men are preprogrammed to behave in a way that promotes their well-being.

If the Common Notions working through the Natural Instinct afford "the first degree of certainty" (103) in human knowledge, discursive thought or reason lies at the opposite end of the scale. Discursive thought "is more liable to error than any of the other faculties" (232). Indeed, "discursive thought has as great a tendency to error as free will to sin" (235).

And people insist on applying this least reliable of the faculties to matters that properly fall within the province of the Common Notions. The very word makes the point: while instinct operates instantaneously, discursive thought runs back and forth (Latin *dis-*

cursus) through a chain of reasoning. The only legitimate function of discursive thought is to apply Common Notions to particular instances (232) by deductive inference (116). But reason must always maintain its dependence on the Common Notions, which are the real source of certainty for man.

Thus "discursive thought is superfluous when a Common Notion is at hand." Nonetheless, "the schools have consistently employed discursive thought throughout their explanations, which is as perverse as putting food in one's ears" (232). Passages bewailing the rash misapplication of discursive thought recur throughout *De Veritate*. To such misapplication Herbert attributes most of the ills of intellectual life.

We are able much more readily to examine principles which are not Common Notions than those which are, although the latter have been given us by nature while the former are casual and external to us. I ascribe this fact to the rash and unconsidered use of discursive thought. Under the influence of wild fictions, ideas of this sort abandon their proper task of applying Common Notions to their furthest limit; while appearing to offer an account of a Common Notion they generally succeed in contradicting it and in transgressing against that fundamental Common Notion which teaches that principles that contradict each other cannot both be true. In this way they destroy belief in the truths of nature itself and substitute sheer inventions, or at least they mix accepted truths with their own vain conceptions so that they lose contact with primary truth. (133)

The elaborate epistemological structure of *De Veritate* was designed to permit Herbert to inveigh reasonably against the abuses of reason.

Discursive thought is undisciplined. All other creatures behave under the spur of necessity or at least uniformly and without deliberation. Man alone has the misfortune, through his tendency to discursive reflection, to be the frequent victim of indecision. At one moment he is rooted in his own prejudices; at the next he is enslaved to those of another; scarcely ever does he succeed in thinking with freedom and candor, nor in listening with humble heart to the voice within him. It is from this source that the confusion by earlier ages of truth with error has arisen and the same process can be witnessed in our own day. Discursive thought wanders among bypaths, often stumbling in its tracks, and when it seeks support from the yielding confusion of truths it brings to the ground its whole crazy structure of principles. Thus man, though bound by birthright only to the law of nature, submits himself to a different code. He transfers his loyalty from the law of nature to the law of religion, and then to civil law, and finally to the rule of his own caprice. And sometimes he bows his neck beneath a yoke so crushing that he can scarcely breathe, though all the while he supports it with smiling countenance. So, after flinging from one altar to another, he finds himself spurned by all and left to follow a hazardous and wandering path. (233–34)

If discursive thought in general "breeds fictions and deceits" (234), it does so especially in the realm of religion. Herbert's solution to the problem is easily stated. "I urge my readers to select, distinguish and arrange these notions, for if the Common Notions are arranged in due order and distinguished from the mass of false opinions, they prevail over mysteries and faith and the arrogance of authority, and enable us to make a clean sweep of fables, error and obscurities" (106).

The Common Notions of religion.   By far the most renowned passages of *De Veritate* appear in the final forty-odd pages. The concluding chapters form the core of Herbert's teaching; they treat point for point—in connection with religion—the topics mentioned in the full title of the volume: *On Truth in Distinction from Revelation, Probability, Possibility, and Error* (69). Herbert formulates his five Common Notions of religion, which would soon be notorious. Then, with the truth of religion in hand, Herbert sets about dismantling what he deems the superstructures of deceit and distortion that have been built up over each of the Common Notions. For one or more Common Notions "exists in every instance of ritual, folly, error and fiction. Upon its foundation the entire structure is built" (268).

The teaching of the five Common Notions constitutes "the true Catholic [i.e., universal] Church, which has never erred" (291). This Church "comprehends all places and all men. . . . And it is only through this Church that salvation is possible" (303). The Common Notions make up "the perfect sphere of the religion of God. . . . If anything is added to it, or taken from it its shape is destroyed, and its perfection ruined" (305–6).[32]

The five points are these: (1) "there is a Supreme God"; (2) "this Sovereign Deity ought to be Worshipped"; (3) the chief element of such worship is the practice of virtue; (4) "vices and crimes . . . must be expiated by repentance"; and (5) "there is a Reward or Punishment after this life" (291–303).

The following section of the book deals with revelation. Herbert plays a careful game, blandly admitting that "revealed truth exists," but adding that "its nature is quite distinct from the truth . . . as I have defined it," in that the latter "is based upon our faculties, while the truth of revelation depends upon the authority of him who reveals it." Herbert argues that a revelation must be made to oneself; "what is received from others as revelation must be accounted not revelation but tradition or history" (308).

As to "those revelations which are solemnly asserted by the priests to have occurred in former ages," Herbert provides a series of criteria by which their proponents may attempt to validate the revelatory status of their texts. The criteria (309–10) would disallow claims for any imaginable text transmitted from ancient times—the Judeo-Christian Bible, for example. One test Herbert prescribes is that when the revelation "had to be written down and transmitted to posterity through the priest's script, it should have been possible fully to correct and restore it in the light of this transcription, in case any addition, omission, or alteration had been made in the succeeding centuries" (309–10). The grave mockery with which Herbert proffers these criteria is unmistakable.

Of course, the criteria do not expressly mention the Christian religion, so Herbert (if pressed) could always say that he was forging a weapon to use against competing religions. But, as Kortholt understood very well, even when Herbert deals explicitly with gentile religion, the same general arguments apply against the corresponding elements of Christian belief.[33] Indeed, the whole point of *De Veritate* is to make the reader see Christianity as one particular religion among many particular religions, none of which can appeal to the reasonable observer. Kortholt may have overstated his case when he proclaimed that Herbert's principal objective was to weaken revealed religion, rather than to establish natural religion; these are two sides of a single coin. But Kortholt was certainly right in reading *De Veritate* as the work of an enemy of Christianity.[34]

The concluding sections of *De Veritate* can be summarized briefly. In Herbert's terminology, probability "signifies the past, possibility the future, and both refer to what is uncertain and unknown" (323). The discussion of probability undercuts reliance on history and tradition. Herbert writes that his belief in God derives, not from history, but from the Common Notions (315). Indeed, Herbert argues, the Common Notions embody a primal religion that far antedates any of the positive religions. He notes that "while ideas which appear to be ancient were once new, when we reflect on their origin, ideas which appear to be new because prejudice hinders a clear understanding of them may actually consist of ancient and even eternal truths." He adds that his own doctrine "was true in every age, though it may appear new to the Reader, and so it must not be taken to be actually new or recent" (320).

Herbert's treatment of possibility undercuts special claims to prophecy. But Herbert insists that virtuous persons can look forward with confidence to eternal blessedness. Otherwise, God would have acted unjustly to implant in man an unfulfillable desire for eternal life. "Is it likely that eternal happiness should be offered to me as an article is offered for sale, and then, just as I am about to purchase it, that the contract should be broken in the manner of a dishonest tradesman? . . . Will not Almighty God abide by His promise as I do by mine?" (329).

The brief discussion of falsity with which the book concludes returns to Herbert's favorite subject, the manifold errors of discursive thought.

Readings of *De Veritate*

Historians of philosophy in this century have located Herbert's ideas in a long tradition that dates back to Greek and Roman antiquity. They have also acknowledged his contribution to the emergence of distinctively modern thought.

Long ago Wilhelm Dilthey pointed to the centrality of Stoic elements in *De Veritate*. "Herbert's doctrine is in essence the attempt to solve the problem of knowledge, especially of religious knowledge, by means of the Stoic doctrine of natural instinct and the common notions."[35] More recently, R. D. Bedford has done justice to the elements of Neoplatonic and Hermetic thought in *De Veritate;* this is the main theme of his book on Herbert.[36]

Perhaps the most striking analysis of Herbert's place in the history of thought is that of Ernst Cassirer. In an essay on Galileo and the concept of truth, Cassirer draws an illuminating comparison between Herbert's philosophy of religion and Galileo's philosophy of science. Cassirer writes, "In the moral domain as in the theoretical, the first and inevitable task proved to be that of separating the necessary from the contingent, the permanent from the variable, the objectively determined from the subjectively imagined." To this end, recourse was had (in the early seventeenth century) to the Stoic philosophy of nature and natural law. Galileo separated the essential from the adventitious in physics in very much the same way that Herbert did in religion. "Just as Galileo proclaimed and defended, as the rule of all physical science, the pure notion of nature, so Herbert installed the same rule in the domain of religious knowledge. In this case too there exists a universal revelation, purely natural, which has no need to prop itself on a text to prove its veracity." Cassirer concludes that a "remarkable accord" exists between *De Veritate* and Galileo's *Il Saggiatore (The Assayer)*, which was published in 1623.[37]

In his own and the following century, however, commentators were less benign in their treatment of Herbert's first book. Not acclaim as a forerunner but scorn as a perverter of religion was Herbert's usual lot. *De Veritate* was placed on the Roman Church's Index of Forbidden Books in 1633. And it was long a favorite target of Protestant divines. As Peter Gay remarks, the Protestant cleric "had every reason to be grateful to the deists, who offered inexhaustible material for the exercise of dialectical skill, sardonic wit, and pious indignation."[38] A good example of such a book is *Natural Religion Insufficient*, which was brought out in 1714 by Thomas Halyburton, a Scottish divine.

Halyburton writes against "this modern Paganism that struts abroad under the modish name of Deism." Halyburton attacks this "paganism a-la-mode," accurately drawing out the implications of the deist position. "They expressly deny any thing to be *fundamental* which has been controverted, or afterwards may be so. In a word, they teach that we are not necessarily to believe any thing, save what is evident to us. And that only is to be reckoned evident, which is confessed by all, and to which nothing that has any appearance of truth can be opposed. Now after this, what is left in *Christianity?*"[39]

Halyburton sees Herbert as the man who put deism into presentable form. Halyburton writes: "This honor he assumes to himself, glories in it, and we see no ground to dispute this with him. I have met with nothing in any of the modern Deists . . . which is not advanced by him, and probably borrowed from his writings." Of *De Veritate* Halyburton says that its argument is "scarcely intelligible to any but metaphysical readers," but deserves attention since its "avowed design" is "to lay a foundation for his peculiar notions in religion." Halyburton specifies, "There are two things at which Herbert . . . plainly aims at—to *overthrow revelation*, and to *establish natural religion* in its room." Although Herbert sometimes seems to speak well of revelation, "this is only . . . a blind to make his reader secure, and fear no danger from the sword that he has under his garment. For . . . he everywhere insinuates prejudices against all revelation, as *uncertain, unnecessary*, and of little or no use to any, save those to whom it was originally . . . given."[40]

Halyburton insists "that his [Herbert's] books aim at the utter subversion of the Christian religion, that his principles overthrow entirely the authority of the scriptures, and are not only inconsistent with, but destructive to the essentials of Christianity. And I further add, that this is everywhere so obvious in his writings, that it will require a strange stretch of charity, to believe our author could be ignorant of it."[41]

Halyburton recognizes a crucial point that is lost in some modern discussions of Herbert—most recently in Bedford's book, in which Herbert is so closely associated with other seventeenth-century thinkers like Milton and Sir Thomas Browne that the radical edge of his doctrine disappears. As Peter Gay explains: "To remote observers, the distance between radical Protestants and deists might seem negligible, but to contemporaries it was decisive. It made all the difference if one accepted revelation, no matter how attenuated, or the Christian God, no matter how remote, or rejected both revelation and the Christian God altogether."[42]

Chapter Three
Later Writings on Religion

In the last decade of his life, Herbert wrote several other works on religion. *De Religione Laici (A Layman's Religion)*, composed 1639–42, was published in the 1645 edition of *De Veritate*. *De Religione Gentilium (The Religion of the Gentiles)*, begun no earlier than 1642, was printed at Amsterdam in 1663; an English version came out in 1705.[1] What is almost certainly Herbert's last book on religion, the bold *Dialogue between a Tutor and his Pupil*, was not published until 1768. By then, the *Dialogue's* skeptical treatment of revealed religion had become commonplace. The historian, though, can recognize in this work Herbert's remarkable anticipation of Enlightenment themes and concerns. The *Dialogue* shows its author's pedagogical procedures at their peak of mastery. Herbert at once taunts the reader into thinking for himself and restrains the reader from uttering too explicitly the dangerous products of that independent thought.

A *Layman's Religion*

Laymen and priests. Herbert's view of religion did not change in the half generation that separates *De Religione Laici* from *De Veritate*. Where the new text differs from its predecessor is in (1) the larger audience it addresses and (2) the greater emphasis it places on the institutional sources of (what Herbert deems) religious mystification.

In *De Veritate*, Herbert wrote for an audience capable of following difficult metaphysical analysis. A contemporary reported that "scarcely one person in a thousand even among the learned" understood the work.[2] In *De Religione Laici*, Herbert addresses the learned, to be sure; only they can read Latin. But he puts his case not as a scholarly epistemologist with a strong metaphysical bent. Rather, he speaks as a layman to other laymen about a problem they share: the choice of a religion.

The other new feature of *De Religione Laici* is its elucidation of motives behind what, in *De Veritate,* Herbert calls the abuses of discursive thought in matters of religion. No doubt the implications of the analysis in *De Veritate* were the same. But now Herbert is as explicit as he could be in blaming the self-promoting machinations of keen-witted and unscrupulous priests for every ill that prevails in organized religion.

The habit of blaming flaws in religion and society upon "priest-craft"—the self-seeking malice of the sacerdotal class—has behind it a long tradition. Cicero's *De Natura Deorum* had as much to tell of the nature of religious abuses as of the nature of the gods; the work served some readers as a veritable handbook of the political abuses of religion. And this theory of a conspiracy on the part of the priestly class to tyrannize the duped laity would become a commonplace of eighteenth-century deist polemics.

It was especially in the seventeenth century that such theories were elaborated. A historian has argued that in the seventeenth century thinkers secularized earlier notions of "man's selfishness, aggression, and unscrupulousness, . . . restating man's sinful propensities as natural human propensities which reason could control but not uproot." Such "doctrines of egoism" provided "motives for the actions of the conspirators and explanations of how and why men were duped." No doubt this way of thinking was encouraged by Reformation disputes, which "made it plausible, even necessary to assume a political motive behind any religious change and often a religious reason behind political demands."[3]

Herbert was a pioneer in his view of history as a conspiracy of the priests against the laity. The seemingly bland title of *De Religione Laici,* in fact, conceals a call to action against the exploiters of decent layfolk everywhere.

The wayfarer. In *De Religione Laici,* Herbert addresses himself to the lay *viator,* the wayfaring pilgrim. This is a familiar Christian image: men ought to live, St. Paul wrote, as "strangers and pilgrims" in this life (Heb. 11:13). Characteristically, Herbert strips the image of any distinctively Christian component.

The opening sentence of the text explains that Herbert is treating "a very serious question. What, namely, shall the layman, encompassed by the terrors of divers churches throughout the world, decide as to the best religion? For there is no church that does not breathe threats, none almost that does not deny the possibility of salvation outside its own pale." How, indeed, "shall he protect himself if every man's individual dogmas about necessary and excellent truth are so proposed as to damn all the rest."[4]

The perplexed *viator* can begin to liberate himself if he recognizes what the priests of the competing religions have in common.

He will find the priestly order, however quarrelsome and clamorous about their faiths, however busy sowing contentions not only among themselves but among neighboring nations, conspiring together none the less about these matters: everywhere to interpose and to maintain their authority; to allow nothing they teach to be so much as doubted; to confine what is most important to abstruse and difficult passages which they interpret; to restrain the most lawful pleasures which they themselves have not appointed; to deny obstinately that heaven can be approached without their influence; to threaten anathemas and eternal punishments against those who differ; briefly, conspiring that neither entering nor leaving this world should be quite lawful without their aid. (123)

With their ceremonies and rituals, the priests "procured splendor to religion, and no mean profit to themselves. Yet while they were in the habit of diverting the soul from virtue to ceremonies and rites, men became bigoted and superstitious rather than good and honest" (107).

According to Herbert, the priests ground their authority on the claim of a special revelation made to or through them. This revelation the laity are asked to accept through the exercise of faith. Herbert, however, insists that "we must either submit to the leadership of Reason or wander in exitless labyrinths" (121).

In place of the particular religions, Herbert would have the wayfarer "first search out doctrines which are analogous to the internal faculties, and afterwards those about which there is most agreement." What he will find are the common notions of religion as presented in *De Veritate:* "the worship of the supreme God by means of every virtue, penitence when we fail therein, and reward or punishment after this life. Those truths therefore that flourish everywhere, and always will flourish, are not confined by the limits of any one religion. For they are divinely inscribed in the understanding itself, and are subject to no traditions written or unwritten. By these truths alone is this universe governed, and disposed to a better state; these therefore consider the catholic truths of the Church" (89–91).

Herbert offers and refutes a possible objection. It may be argued "that if the people are steadfast only in the catholic truths something at least will be lost to religion. Perhaps. But nothing, certainly, will be lost to a pious life or to virtue; yet by virtue is God so well worshipped that I have called that religion the best which is best squared to its rule" (109). Few readers can miss the sneer directed at what usually passes for religion.

Most of Herbert's rhetoric in *De Veritate* has for its target religion in this sense, especially what Herbert thinks of as the priestly class in general. In a few passages he is more specific, turning his sarcasm against the Judeo-Christian tradition. Of course, he does so with considerable care. At one point, for example, he makes what at first seems a broad concession to the distinctiveness of the Christian Bible among the sacred texts of mankind. "Our European will find conspicuous above the rest, both in antiquity and in extraordinary authority, the Sacred Scriptures communicated to the Jews, and by them to the Gentiles. To these, therefore, he may give complete faith in all things which, on the authority of the [particular] Church, are said to have been done in former times." With a characteristic movement of thought, Herbert (a few sentences later) blandly cancels the apparent concession.

On this condition, however, that there be a common privilege of studying and of arriving at conclusions about the consequences of acts said to have taken place from the earliest ages of the world, and that, although faith in the historical narrative remains the Church's prerogative, the liberty of passing judgment shall remain with mankind. Quite wondrous matters, certainly, are recorded in the Sacred Scriptures more than in all other histories, wonders however which do not dull the mind, but exercise or sharpen it. But the Church will see about these, which indeed I should never have learned had it kept silent, or believed but for its testimony. (99)

Nothing here is explicitly unorthodox. (A traditional view of faith saw it as confidence in what was—to earthly reason—impossible.) Yet every word of the passage breathes mockery of the religious tradition in which Herbert was raised.

For Herbert, the only real authority—the only system of belief and practice that can win a reasonable layman's uncompelled adherence—is that of the primal religion in whose reality he so fervently believed. For "Divine Providence, truly, remains everywhere the same . . . [and] the doctrine of catholic truths has never been novel" (103–5). Following these catholic truths of *De Veritate* will, Herbert writes, abolish controversy and put a spur to the exercise of virtue (127).

The Ancient Religion of the Gentiles

The Greek and Roman deities were known to every person of learning in the Renaissance. The multiplicity of these gods and the frequently unsavory conduct in which they were reported to have engaged presented a problem to a thinker of Herbert's stripe. He was committed to the existence of a primal religion of perfect purity and simplicity.

In *De Religione Gentilium* Herbert approaches the question in this way.[5] He grants that much of the pagans' religion is a tissue of absurdities. Yet he asks "whether amongst those Heaps of Ethnical [i.e., pagan] Superstitions, a Thread of Truth might be found, by the assistance of which it was possible for them to extricate themselves out of that *Labyrinth* of Error, in which they were involved" (3). The strands of that thread prove to be the "five undeniable Propositions" first set forth in *De Veritate*. Holding fast to these, "the most perspicacious amongst the Heathens got out of this *Labyrinth*" (4).

In short, Herbert concludes "for an established truth, That the Religion of the Ancient Heathens was not so absurd and stupid as is generally imagined" (270). The wiser among the heathens had distinguished the pentad of undeniable notions from "the dirt and Rubbish in which they lay" (367). Of course, they often did so silently, for "it was a very bold Attempt in all Ages to reject what the Sacerdotal Order had introduced into Religion from their Traditions or Revelations." The wiser sort recognized that "it was much better for them to doubt than to deny" (356).

Source. Herbert drew most of the scholarly information in *De Religione Gentilium* from a massive Latin work published in 1641 by Gerard Vos (or Vossius), a Dutch theologue and friend of Grotius. Vos's *Of Gentile Theology and Christian Physiology, or of the Origin and Progress of Idolatry* is a work of vast learning but scant unity. A recent scholar labels its author "a bottomless sink of miscellaneous erudition."[6] D. C. Allen, understandably weary from slogging through this work and many other Renaissance treatises on mythology, writes that Vos "ran down the scale of idolatry from the veneration of famous men to the religious cultivation of cicadas and onions. Thoroughly skilled in all branches of science too, he writes full zoological descriptions of the nature and habits of each creature as he descends the ladder of idols from elephants to poisonous insects. There is little about shellfish that he can be told by those who fear and pray to the oyster."[7]

"The learned Vossius" (as Herbert calls him [12]) devotes much of his extensive treatment of ancient mythology to the pursuit of a scholarly diversion that was common practice among Renaissance scholars, though one that Vos takes to extremes. This is the systematic identification of members of the Greek and Roman pantheon with alleged counterparts in the Bible. Thus, in Saturn Vos sees the Hebrew Noah; a few pages later, however, so free is the method, he can suggest that "the patriarch Abraham was worshipped in Saturn."[8]

The general point is that Vos provides an explanation for the analogies to be found between pagan myths and the Bible. Vos sees these as products of pagan borrowing and debasing of the original truths that lie within the Judeo-Christian tradition. What elements of truth the pagans took from revealed wisdom have been corrupted by the weakness of human reason and the endless machinations of Satan.[9] In Vos's view, the religion of the pagans did not suffice to win salvation.

Although he borrowed data from Vos wholesale (often, though by no means always, with acknowledgment), Herbert could not have differed more sharply in intention from the apologetic Dutchman. Herbert held that salvation comes through the common notions—and these are (by definition) common to paganism and Christianity, except insofar as these have been corrupted by "the Religious Cheat of the Priests" (319). Far from the usual defense of Christianity as the true ground of whatever shadowy verities can be seen in pagan traditions, Herbert's tightly written little treatise offers what a hostile eighteenth-century scholar rightly called "an elaborate apology for Paganism."[10] In the words of D. C. Allen, "Herbert rejects previous theories by asserting that Christian rites and ethics, when seemingly followed by non-Christians, are not the consequences of imitation but of natural reasoning."[11]

Herbert's *De Religione Gentilium* is a bold and provocative piece of writing. One would be hard-pressed to think of another book of its day in which views held by such notorious anti-Christian polemicists of antiquity as Celsus and Julian the Apostate are explicitly endorsed (299, 386). It is little wonder that during the first decade of the eighteenth century Herbert's treatise found its place on the Index of Forbidden Books, along with *De Veritate.*

The history of religion. Clement Webb may well be correct in his assessment of the intellectual roots of Herbert's theory of religious history. "For Herbert, as for many since his time, the belief of the Protestant Reformers that Christianity had been perverted from its original purity and simplicity through the multiplication by an interested priesthood of traditions calculated to exalt their own dignity and increase their influence, was generalized into a theory of the corruption of primitive religion by priests."[12]

To cite Heinrich Scholz's crisp formulation, Herbert held that "in every historical [i.e., positive] religion one must distinguish carefully between its reasonable origin and its unreasonable development. God's universal revelation through reason and the world— for which no history is needed—constitutes the source of every historical religion." But in every case, priests have supplemented this "reasonable core" with unreasonable practices and beliefs. "Thus the whole history of religion is a process of depravation due to the malice of the priesthood. The overall conclusion to be drawn is this: whatever in the historical religions is true, is not historical; and whatever in them is historical, is not true."[13]

Vos had been rather vague in his explanation of what Herbert calls "that luxuriant Progress of Religion" (192) as it unfolds into polytheism and idolatry. Herbert, in contrast, could not be clearer in his causal account of that "progress." At every step, Herbert asks: in whose interest is this elaboration of rite and story? In each instance, the answer is the same: the fault lies in "the crafty Contrivance of the Priests" (73).

Of course, little in Herbert's acidly anticlerical account of the history of religion will stand up to twentieth-century scrutiny. But the interpretation Herbert works out would be an influential one in the development of a critical theory of religion. Moreover, from a literary standpoint, the story he tells stands on its own as a marvelously comic one-sided recounting of the unfolding in time of the positive religions. Nothing, after all, is more amusing than a clever villain, and no villains are more nefariously cunning than Herbert's sacerdotal cheats.

Why did polytheism emerge? Herbert answers: The priests

"thought they could embarrass the Minds of the People more with the Notion of Plurality of Deities, than by the Worship of One only . . . especially after they had invented and dispersed a different way of Worship for each of them. They also expected to reap more Profit, and have larger Stipends from the various Rites, Ceremonies and Sacred Mysteries which they contrived and divulged, than if Men of all Ages should continue to perform the same Duties of piety and Virtue" (271).

Why is it that "the same God signifies often different things, and on the contrary, different Names are often applied to the same thing"? This state of affairs, Herbert replies, "proceeds from the Priests' Explaining their Mysteries in different Countries, according to their own Interest and Humour, or to make them Intelligible to the People" (138).

Why were the names of the pagan gods so "very much confounded"? One reason Herbert gives, quite plausibly, is that among the ancient writers "every one endeavored as much as they could to strain the different words of several Countries to their own sense" (60). Such local or nationalistic factors are often adduced in *De Religione Gentilium,* as in this passage: "The Gods were so numerous amongst the Heathens, that not only every Region and Province, but every island and almost little River, had their own Country Deities, lest they should seem to be out-done by their Neighbours" (184).

What about the absurd fables told of the gods—the abundant thefts and rapes laid to their account? Herbert explains that "the Original of these Fables, was thus: There being many Jupiters, Mars's, Venus's and Bacchus's, in several Ages, and different Parts of the World; and at that time, some Men advanced amongst the Number of the Gods: Some in favor of their own Country Deities Ridicule those of the other, and they in requital were as free with theirs" (162).

In another passage, Herbert rehearses the arguments that "the Priests at that time offered in Vindication of their Lascivious Deities." Some of the "abominable things . . . related of the Heathen Gods" are "Poetical Fictions, invented to expose the Gods of some other Country." Anyway, "all things were lawful for the Gods"; and their amorous dealings with mortals begot "Heroes, who far exceeded our weak and frail Natures, and came into the World for some good and great End." Here Herbert yields, as he often does

in the treatise, to the temptation to let the wheedling priests speak
in their own defense. Their superficially plausible, but fundamen-
tally ridiculous, explanations form comic high points of the book.
Such is the energy of the priestly voice that Herbert has to break
in to silence it. The passage just quoted concludes with Herbert
noting that some of the priests' arguments "may pass as pleasant
Excuses, yet others are so absurd and ridiculous, that not only
discover the Frailties of the Gods, but seem designed to cover and
conceal the Libidinous Wickedness of Men" (179).

   Paganism and Christianity.   In his book *The Ancient Theology,*
D. P. Walker devotes a chapter to *De Religione Gentilium.* He argues
that Herbert, like Bruno and Campanella before him, was an ad-
herent of "the good old astral religion": that is, of Platonic-Hermetic
star-worship.[14] Walker's is a learned essay, rich in the esoteric Renaissance lore one has come to expect from scholars at the Warburg
Institute. Unfortunately, little in Herbert's book supports Walker's
contention.

   Insofar as Herbert had an unexpressed underlying concern in *De
Religione Gentilium,* it is with Christianity. As a historian of deism
writes, in this treatise "Herbert's attacks were upon heathen religious
books, heathen sacrifices, heathen miracles and other features of
heathen religions which he characterized as corruptions of the original and pure religion of nature. Yet the wording of these attacks
was such as to make the reader feel that the author had the Bible
and historic Christianity in mind." The historian specifies that "Herbert's discussion of the subject of sacrifice is written as though
directed against that element in heathen religions. But his statements are of such an inclusive character as . . . evidently [to]
include in his condemnation the sacrifices of the Old Testament
and the widely held Christian doctrine of the propitiatory sacrifice
of Christ. Yet so guarded were his statements that if he were attacked
for them he could claim . . . simply [to be] opposing heathen
doctrines and practices or such abuses in the Christian church as
Luther had criticized when he protested against the selling of in-
dulgences."[15] This twentieth-century scholar, John Orr, is reading
Herbert precisely as Kortholt did. The seventeenth-century theology
professor noted how remarks in *De Religione Gentilium* ostensibly
concerned with paganism really "touch upon" Christianity criti-
cally.[16] No doubt this is how Herbert intended his text to be read.

   Numerous passages in the book beg to be read as malign sideswipes at Christianity. A good example appears in one of the lengthy "specious Discourses" with "neither Solidity nor Truth in them" that Herbert feigns to have been spoken by the pagan priests in defense of their "System of Theology" (290 [mispaginated as 299]). They explain the need for propitiating the "men, admitted into Heaven" who will serve as "mediators between [God] and Mortals"(288). Of course, deism rejects any form of mediation between God and men, while Christianity centers upon such mediation. The line of defense here would be for Herbert to say that he was satirizing abusive worship of saints—a common Protestant complaint against the Roman Church.

Herbert's mockery can surface in unexpected places, as in this discussion of Roman iconography: "They also represent [Jupiter] an Infant sucking, and he and his Sister Juno sitting in Fortune's Lap, greedy after the Breast; yet the Matrons of Rome had then a most profound Veneration for him, as Cicero says. But I am of opinion he was the first God that the Ancients ever adored bawling in a cradle, before he had performed any noble Exploit; for they could not be very fond of such a snivelling Deity" (191). Few readers will miss the irreverent analogy implied here.

Of course, Herbert nowhere makes his case against Christianity explicit. At one point he does go so far as to explain the need for composing an apology for paganism. The church fathers, he says, "were the Heathens' most inveterate Enemies." The early Christians did everything they could in their writings to make paganism seem absurd. "They pass by the more certain and Orthodox parts of [the pagans'] Religion in silence, and from their Superstitions and Rites, take an occasion to utter severe Invectives against them, and represent them after a most ridiculous manner" (291).

The polemical point of *De Religione Gentilium* is to do justice to the pagan religion that has been (Herbert believes) thus tendentiously misrepresented by Christian authors. Herbert has turned the Christian interpretation of paganism on its head. Rather than finding distorted shards of Christianity in the non-Christian systems of religion, Herbert professes to find in *The Ancient Religion of Gentiles* a standard against which to measure Christianity and find it wanting.

D. C. Allen writes: "In a way Herbert's posthumous book marked the beginning of the end for the whole theory that etymological investigations and comparative biographies would show the Old Testament behind all other religious theory and history. The mon-

omania that plagued so many Christian scholars was being cured."[17]
To be sure, Christian scholars would not hesitate to accuse Herbert
of monomania in finding his beloved five common notions wherever
he looked, even in what he called "that wonderful Hodg-potch of
Religion, contrived and patched up by the Priests" of ancient Greece
and Rome (357).

A Dialogue between a Tutor and His Pupil

The question of authenticity.   In 1768 a London bookseller
published a work that he attributed on internal evidence to Edward
Herbert. Most scholars have accepted the first editor's judgment.
Hutcheson writes: "Herbert's authorship of the *Dialogue* seems to
me unquestionable. The peculiarities of his thought and style are
so marked on every page that for anyone else to have written the
book would have required a miracle of imitation."[18]

In 1942, however, Mario Rossi argued that the book was not
from Herbert's pen. He observed that the harshly anti-Christian
polemic of the *Dialogue* was not typical of Herbert. He also asserted
that the dialogue form was "alien to Herbert's mentality."[19]

On Herbert's "mentality," Rossi is simply wrong; the present
volume as a whole shows that the interplay of multiple voices is
characteristic of Herbert's writing throughout his career. As to the
greater explicitness of Herbert's hostility to the Christian religion,
that is hardly surprising in the only vernacular book Herbert composed on the philosophy of religion. In the *Dialogue,* Herbert addresses not his learned European contemporaries, but English readers
of the future.

For it is a safe bet that Herbert did not intend the *Dialogue* to
be published in his lifetime. He never mentions this book in his
published works, and when the manuscript was being prepared for
the press the Herbert family reported that they had never heard of
a "composition . . . bearing that title."[20] No wonder, for this is
Herbert's boldest statement on religion, a text of "astounding au-
dacity and . . . sarcasm," in the words of Charles Lyttle. That
critic calls the *Dialogue* "Herbert's most remarkable work. . . .
More clearly, more explicitly and in better literary form than in any
other of his works, it gives his religious philosophy and its practical
bearings."[21]

Rossi's arguments against the book's authenticity have been carefully answered by Gawlick (xvi–xxvi). The reader of Herbert need not be denied the pleasure of exploring this remarkable *Dialogue,* every page of which, as Gawlick puts it, is "stamped with the spirit of the Enlightenment" (v).

The uses of dialogue. The dialogue form enables Lord Herbert to enact the drama of enlightenment. The Tutor speaks in a reasonable voice; throughout the work he provides the Pupil, not just with information, but with a framework for looking at the phenomenon of religion. Again and again, the Tutor tests the youth's understanding of that framework. Again and again, the young man passes the test, but pushes onward to a dangerously overexplicit critique of established religion. At this point the Tutor typically draws the Pupil back with a gesture of what Lyttle calls "ironical deference to the judgment of 'our learned divines.' "[22]

A typical example of the Tutor's double-edged concessions to religious authority (63–64) would be too long to quote here. A brief passage will have to do. The Pupil has just referred to the various opinions maintained "in several parts of Christendom" over the nature of Christ's presence in the sacramental bread. The Tutor urges the youth to remember "that where the text is not clear, your best ground will be the authority of the church, and the practice of the most ancient times; but then again which authority, and which church you should adhere to, will be another question" (251). The turn of thought after the semicolon is representative of the Tutor's duplicitously diplomatic rhetoric throughout the work. The piously deferential gesture sets up—and protects against the consequences of—the succeeding thrust.

At several points in the *Dialogue,* the Tutor assumes the voice of the hated priests. Advancing the arguments that the Pupil will encounter in the world, the Tutor tests the boy's readiness to defend the deist position. The Tutor presses the debate. "The priests, I conceive, would answer you thus" (97); "the priests, I believe, would reply" (98); "the priests would assuredly reply" (99).

The Tutor is putting pressure on the Pupil to see if he has outgrown what eighteenth-century thinkers would call his nonage. The drama of Herbert's *Dialogue* arises not from any fundamental disagreement between the interlocutors; they differ only in the young man's greater impetuosity and correspondingly greater openness in attacking established religion. The drama comes in seeing the boy assimilate the Tutor's cannily duplicitous mode of utterance. A key element of that mode is the use of Herbert's favorite stalking-horse: the lay status that exempts the sniper at religion from engaging in pitched battles on theological niceties.

In one notable passage early in the book, Herbert puts into the Pupil's mouth a comparison that has a great deal to say about the significance of dialogic form. "I do conceive with you, that nature is but God's servant, and may be aptly compared to a young scholar, who learning to write the characters of the alphabet, is guided in the forming them by an excellent master, who holds his hand, whilst thus the characters, which he could not otherwise draw, seem thus to be his own" (51). The passage serves as an emblem of the work as a whole. Like Nature, the Pupil stands in need of guidance, in his case to master an artificial system of discourse. For natural religion must be taught in a guardedly indirect way. And the Tutor of natural religion allows his young charge to educate himself by appropriation: making "his own" the mode of thought in which he is being trained. Implicitly, Herbert invites every reader to work through that same process: moving from the role of Pupil to that of Tutor.

The sacrifice of Abraham. The ideas presented in the *Dialogue* will not surprise the student of Herbert's earlier writings on religion, though the boldness of their expression may. Two examples will establish the point, one early in the work, one late.

Asked by the Pupil why he seems to make little distinction between "ancient philosophers and priests," the Tutor replies: "Before religion, (i.e.) rites, ceremonies, pretended revelations, and the like were invented, there was no worship of God but in a rational way, whereof the philosophers pretending to be masters, did to this end not only teach virtue and piety, but were great examples of it in their lives, whom also the people chiefly followed, till they gave ear to the covetous and crafty sacerdotal order" (42–43). This is indeed an apology for paganism—for pagan philosophy, precisely— more direct than anything in *De Religione Gentilium*.

In that earlier book, as was shown above, Herbert often relies upon his reader to make a comparison (implicit in the text) between pagan and Christian religion. In the *Dialogue,* the Tutor and Pupil explicitly pursue such analogies, not once but repeatedly. Thus on successive pages the Pupil remarks: "The priests among the Gentiles made believe as strange things as Christ's passion though in another kind"; and "the heathens would find some things as hard to believe in our religion, as we find in theirs" (241, 242). This is not mere relativism; the ironies are clearly directed at the religion of the interlocutors' own culture.

The single most provocative passage in the *Dialogue* remains to be mentioned. It is that in which the two men discuss the divine command to Abraham to sacrifice his son Isaac (Gen. 22). As Günter Gawlick shows, Lord Herbert would seem to have formulated first what would become a standard critical approach to this most perplexing Old Testament episode.[23] The two key paragraphs merit quotation in full.

> *Pupil:* I must needs acknowledge that the offering of men, and particularly of children by their parents, was a most horrid and detestable sacrifice, so that I did never read, without astonishment, in the holy writ, where it is said that God commanded Abraham to offer his son Isaac, as an holocaust, or burnt offering, and that Abraham without any dispute or enquiry whether the voice came from God, resolved presently to render a prompt obedience thereunto; and after he had pretended to his young men or servants, that he went about another business, and to his son that he meant to offer another sacrifice, did yet really purpose to kill his said son, by way of an oblation to God. All which our priests, not only maintain to be well done upon these terms, but reproach them with want of faith, who believe otherwise. I would fain to know your opinion what a rational man should do in such a case, suppose we heard a strange voice now commanding us to kill one another, what should I think of it?
>
> *Tutor:* This question is from our purpose, howbeit I will give you the best answer I can, in the quality of a rational person, without interesting myself in the revelations and mysteries of theological schools: I say then, that according to the dictates of common reason, I should believe that this voice came rather from some wicked spirit, than from God; all homicide, particularly that of a parent's destroying his own child with his own hands, without any offense given by him, being so repugnant to the laws of God and nature, that it is not credible that the Deus, Optimus, Maximus, should be the author of such a precept, as was contradictory to his other pious Commandments, mentioned in the holy writ. For though I must confess, the ten commandments of the decalogue were not at that time extant in tables of stone,

> yet because without all question, the divine grace was ever
> extant, and operative in men's hearts, I cannot but extremely
> wonder, that Abraham being a wise and learned man, should
> believe that the voice came from the great and wise God;
> unless, at the same time, God had constrained him to the
> belief thereof, by some such irresistible power, as Abraham
> knew not how to contradict it. (77–78)

Of course, this last evasion on the Tutor's part will not stand up
for a moment. The Pupil notes that God was (according to the
Biblical text) tempting Abraham, and "it is an improper manner
of speaking, to say that a temptation is made to any, whose will is
not free . . . that he may give either his affirmative or negative
voice as he please." Abraham, the young man concludes, "might
have used other means, than it seems by the text he did, to discover
the truth of the voice, and the goodness of the precept, which was
represented to him" (78–79). Rather than an irrational hero of faith,
Abraham ought to have been a deist, testing an allegedly divine
command against those eternal verities that not even the divinity
could countermand.

No other episode in the Bible so sharply puts forward the anti-
nomy of reason and faith. That is why Kierkegaard (in *Fear and
Trembling*) selected the Abraham story as the emblem of his philosophy of faith. At the other end of the spectrum of religious opinion,
Edward Herbert first worked out the skeptical rationalist reading
of the episode, a reading that became a familiar one in the Enlightenment period.

That rationalist (a Kierkegaardian would say, shallowly ration-
alizing) view of Abraham's gesture of faith would be the target of
Kierkegaard's assault. A great deal hung on the reading of the
episode. As Gawlick explains, "Up to the seventeenth century the
accepted view was that ethics was founded on religion." In that
age, "it dawned upon the thoughtful that there must be moral
obligations antecedent to, and independent of, divine revelation."[24]
The passage just cited from Herbert's *Dialogue* marks a key moment
in that process of separating ethics (Herbert would have said virtue)
from any necessary dependence upon revealed religion.

Chapter Four
Herbert as Historian

Both of Edward Herbert's volumes of history bear dedications to King Charles I. Each was evidently undertaken at royal behest. In each instance Herbert found himself obliged to make a case to which he was by no means fully committed. Hence the "satirical tone which pervades" the books and "the witty distance at which Herbert keeps himself from his subject."[1] The hasty or superficial reader will find in such a book an apologetic narrative; the careful reader will notice the qualifying elements of irony and of deadpan ridicule. The delicate balancing act of writing simultaneously for both readers produced some of Herbert's finest prose. Both books can be read for entertainment, as well as for the political lessons that Renaissance theory expected history to provide. Indeed, the alert reader will be drawn by the author's irony toward the political judgment that the book leaves for the reader to formulate.

The Expedition to the Isle of Rhé

The historical background.   In his dedicatory epistle to the king, Herbert calls the charge (first given him by the duke of Buckingham) of writing *The Expedition* a "heavy burden" that he "could by no excuse avoid."[2] It is easy to understand his reluctance: all observers then and since have recognized the mission to Rhé as a fiasco for the English.

The bungling royal favorite, the duke of Buckingham, had in the summer of 1627 taken a force of eight thousand men to the Isle of Rhé off La Rochelle on the western coast of France. The Huguenots whom they had come to support proved reluctant comrades. And the French troops whom they blockaded in the fortress of St. Martin waited them out. Short of food and water (the English had poisoned their wells), the besieged Frenchmen were at last compelled to ask for terms of surrender. Incredibly, instead of drawing up terms "on the spot . . . . the Duke merely professed his admiration for the courage of the garrison, gave assurances that he would treat them

well, and invited the deputy to come back on the following day."
(The quotations are from a modern biographer of Buckingham who
is very well disposed toward his subject.) The next day, Buckingham
gave the returned French deputy three hours to draw up his own
terms. When the man "replied that he would need at least twenty-
four hours to prepare his conditions," Buckingham granted the extra
day.[3] Before that deadline had arrived, though, outside help reached
the French garrison. The blockade was broken, the French repro-
visioned, and the English were now the besieged. After several futile
and avoidable engagements undertaken by Buckingham to salvage
his honor, the English straggled home in November. They had lost
five thousand men, and many of the survivors were badly injured.

English public opinion was provoked by the disaster on what was
called "the Isle of Rue." Sir Simonds D'Ewes reports that Buckingham's "coming safe home occasioned almost as much sorrow as
the slaughter and perishing of all the rest." Rumors flew about
alleging treason on Buckingham's part. It was said that "the whole
campaign had been so managed as to give the impression that it
was a protestant crusade when in reality it was part of a popish
plot." Many agreed with a poem going around that charged Buckingham with "treachery, neglect and cowardice."[4]

Buckingham was assassinated in August 1628 (to no one's surprise but the king's), and Herbert reports himself content at that
time to "sacrifice to Privacy and silence" the "loose sheets" entrusted
to him by Buckingham as the basis for a defense of the mission.
The French, however, "so puffed up with their good successes,"
began publishing accounts of the incident that took "occasion thereupon to wrong the universal honor of this Nation" (xxix–xxx). So
Herbert felt obliged to take up the abandoned project and defend
the indefensible. He completed one version that he presented in
1630 to the king; in 1632 he presented final versions in both English
and Latin (the latter for an international readership). Neither was
published in his lifetime, although the work offers "an outstanding
blend of competent historical analysis with vivid journalism."[5] The
king may have come to share Herbert's initial preference to let the
affair sink from sight.

   The book.   As Rossi notes in an early article, Herbert's ar-
guments in The Expedition to Rhé "consist principally of insults."[6]
Many are directed against Jacob Isnard, who in 1629 published a
Latin account of the French victory at Rhé. Impugning the motives

of "cackling Isnard" (124), disputing with him points of the historical record, Herbert in particular goes out of his way to mock the Frenchman's errors in Latin diction, especially his misuse of ancient Latin terms to refer to different modern things. Such polemic was commonplace in Renaissance Latin writing throughout the seventeenth century.

While Herbert nails Isnard to the wall on small points of usage, he accepts his judgment on the central action of the campaign, that is, Buckingham's negligence in not promptly laying down terms of surrender for the French garrison. Herbert reports Isnard's view. "The Supreme Arbiter of all things, that he might deliver the besieged from that great danger, so blinded the sense and mind of the enemy, that, in an affair so sudden and opportune, as nothing could be more hurtful than delay, he yet did seek occasion of deferring it." At this physical and moral center of his book (141), Herbert comments blandly, "Isnard is not here much mistaken, for it seems the divine Providence could not, or at least ought not, do more."

Herbert's handling of Isnard points up his treatment of Buckingham, the one being the inverse or photographic negative of the other. Taking issue with the "cackling" Frenchman on every philological nicety and small point of interpretation, Herbert nonetheless grants Isnard his central and deciding judgment. With Buckingham, Herbert offers a defense on many details, but gradually builds up in the reader's mind a conviction of the duke's ineptitude and culpability.

Thus Herbert's elaborate game of philological and historical dueling with Isnard has real purpose to it. Quite different is the duke of Buckingham's absurd preoccupation with politeness and chivalric decorum. A major theme of *The Expedition* is that the duke treats all aspects of the campaign as matters of personal honor—which he will defend at the cost of any number of English lives. Sooner or later the reader catches the mockery with which Herbert views the duke's fatal obsession with politesse.

After transcribing in English and French pages of the "most courteous letters" exchanged between the duke and the commander of the besieged French garrison, Herbert writes, "Briefly, businesses were then so carried, as somebody said, the friendship seemed serious, and war but for pastime and exercise only" (106–7). After the breaking of the English blockade, Herbert's mockery comes closer to the surface. "It grieved my Lord Duke of Buckingham now that he had showed this facility, for he knew at last Clemency did become a Commander, but not before the enemy was already overthrown" (156). Few readers could miss Herbert's indirect but damning explanation of why Buckingham fought a futile battle in a lost cause. "Now there was no occasion to stay but such as would have affrighted away any other; that is, my Lord Duke of Buckingham was ashamed to depart now the enemy drew near, and so much the rather as their number was greater" (199). And the sarcasm is overwhelming when Herbert reports the last action of the English before reembarking for home. "The question now among the Colonels was who should last go a shipboard, as taking this to be a special point of Honor. This controversy was ended by casting of lots, so much leisure had we now even for recreation and pastime" (266–67).

As for the fighting itself, Buckingham's generalship put the English in a position where "neither on the one side we could conveniently fight nor handsomely retire on the other" (168). In a somber passage whose rhythmic power places it with his finest efforts in prose, Herbert records the inevitable outcome.

Although my Lord Duke of Buckingham from the beginning of the combat exhorted them equally to maintain the reputation of their Country, yet a fit place to give proof of their valor being wanting, all his speech was but in vain. But neither succeeded it well that our men did not seem all of one mind; for whilst some strive to run away, and others again hindered them, they mutually acted the part of enemies to each other. Thus as in troops they labored to pass the bridge (which had no rails or fences on either side) one might observe these thrusting forward, and others putting them back, until their weapons falling out of their hands, and grappled together, they fell arm in arm into the sea. (245–46)

The slaughter was so great because "there was no means to distinguish friends from enemies" (247)—a pregnant remark indeed.

In the concluding chapter of the book, Herbert offers his final reply to "the rash folly of Isnard" (281). He writes that throughout the campaign "there was enough done for honor, too much for effusion of blood on either part. Let both Nations, therefore, have their due glory" (283). Nevertheless, he goes on to defend English honor in particular, returning to a point he had made earlier when he had asked who, like the French, "would have killed men fallen down and sticking in the mud?" Accordingly, he had gone on to inquire, "Was it not more dishonorable to vanquish thus than to be vanquished?" (257). Hence, Herbert can claim, "Our victories were masculine, glorious, and due to our virtue," while "yours was only opportune, obnoxious, and momentary" (284–85). Rising to paradox in his last pages, Herbert contends that "if it be granted that the French did triumph over the vanquished, it must not be denied but the English triumphed over the Victory itself" (286). He concludes on a milder note, reproving disputatious "wranglers" and urging, "Let it be lawful for every one to defend the dignity of his Country, unlawful for any to sow or nourish the seeds of dissention" (287). In other words, do not kick a country when it is down—a worthy sentiment, but hardly a defense of Buckingham. Herbert is in the same predicament as Buckingham's poor soldiers: "exhorted . . . to maintain the reputation of their Country," but deprived of a "fit place" or topic of argument for doing so.

For all its vigor and somber mockery, *The Expedition* will never have many readers. Its subject is too special, too small. But it merits discussion as the book in which Herbert worked out the techniques of writing history in two voices, the blandly apologetic and the covertly mocking—a technique he would develop further in his masterly book on Henry VIII.

The Life and Reign of King Henry the Eighth

"It took its first beginning from Your Majesty's particular . . . commands," Herbert wrote in dedicating *The Life and Reign* to King Charles.[7] Herbert started work on the project in 1632 and completed most of his writing by 1638. The book was published in 1649, the year after his death, and has several times been reprinted. It quickly established its place as a classic of English history. In his *Some Thoughts Concerning Reading and Study for a Gentleman,* John Locke lists as "those who are accounted to have writ best particular parts of our English history . . . Bacon, of Henry VII and Herbert of Henry VIII."[8]

Developments in history writing. *The Life and Reign* bears the marks of several developments in Renaissance historiography. First to be noticed is the reliance on, and extensive citation of, primary documents and official papers. As J. R. Hale has written, the generation of historians up to Herbert's friend John "Selden established once and for all that documents and not secondary authorities are the essential foundation of reliable history."[9] Herbert goes out of his way to mock earlier romanticized versions of events. Thus, after transcribing and translating a papal letter having to do with Henry's contested divorce, Herbert wrote: "After the commission was read, our chronicles say, the king was called and appeared . . . personally in court, at whose feet the queen prostrated herself, demanding justice, right, and pity, etc. But now to come to the authentick record." Herbert proceeds to record what the documents say (369). His sources for the book were both royal archives and the private collection of Sir Robert Cotton.

Repeatedly stressing his "free and impartial" (585) stance as a historian, Herbert grants the reader freedom to judge for himself or herself. In a typical passage Herbert writes, "I will only lay down the particulars, as far as by records, or otherwise I could gather them, remitting the rest to the equal reader" (567). (*Equal* probably means both "impartial" and "having the capacity to judge.") This is a familiar assertion in Renaissance history writing. Johannes Sleidan, a sixteenth-century historian of the Reformation whom Herbert (in a rare note of esteem) calls "the discreet and diligent Sleidan" (554), had written, "I do not add anything of my own, nor do I make any judgment on [the facts], but willingly and freely leave it to my reader."[10] Just how impartial Herbert actually was will be considered below; his stance or pose was that of an unprejudiced researcher.

English examples also lie behind Herbert's way of writing history. Of particular significance is the group of authors whom modern scholars call "the politic historians." The most celebrated of these are Walter Ralegh and Francis Bacon, whose *History of the Reign of King Henry VII* furnished the principal model for Herbert's study of the next Henry. The politic historians sharply distinguished true history from the chronicle histories that were still being written. In those they saw mere lumber rooms of undigested and unanalyzed data occasionally interrupted by edifying sermonettes on the fall of the mighty. Condemning "monks or closet penmen" as poor examples to follow, Bacon wrote that "it is for ministers and great officers to judge of these things, and those who have handled the helm of government, and been acquainted with the difficulties and mysteries of state business." For Bacon, the historian's "is a task of great labor and judgment": "to place as it were before the eyes, the revolutions of times, the characters of persons, the fluctuations of counsels, the courses and currents of actions, the bottoms of pretences, and the secrets of governments."[11]

Herbert's book follows this 'Baconian prescription. Like Bacon's *Henry VII*, *The Life and Reign* "joins the methods of the ordinary chronicler to those of the politic historian."[12] The reader today may be struck by the abundance of chroniclelike features: not just the annalistic framework, but the mechanical transitions ("Let us look a while upon foreign business" [645]) and the compilation of diverse information. But the reader should not miss the "politic" elements of *The Life and Reign:* the knowing analysis of court doings, the shrewd generalization, the insidiously damning character sketch. For Herbert, as for Bacon, history is no longer an embodied confirmation of moral commonplaces; it is an advanced textbook in political analysis. As S. L. Goldberg writes (quoting Ralegh), "For the 'politic' historian, to write history was to call the past to a political judgment, 'judiciously consider the defects in counsel, or obliquity in proceeding,' and hence to seek the motives and circumstances of action."[13]

Another feature of *The Life and Reign* merits placement in the historiographic tradition. Like Bacon, Herbert followed ancient historians in inventing speeches to convey what must have been said in a given circumstance but has not survived in the records.[14] Herbert's availing himself of this procedure may give grounds for surprise. After all, he was not above attacking the Catholic polemicist Cardinal Pole for "pretend[ing] (in more than one place) to have known even so much as the king's thoughts (by revelation)" (402). The distinction in Herbert's mind may well have been between the spoken, which is public, and therefore deducible from the historical record; and the thought, which belongs to that private realm to which access is unavailable, though claimed by the charlatan.

A few of Herbert's invented speeches fulfill another function, this one peculiar to his book of history. At points of particular importance, when he wanted to state his own view but was reluctant to do so directly, he would devise a fictitious personage. This figure, quite unattested in the historical record, is identified as (to give a pair of examples) "one who was zealous of God's honor and the public good" (178) or "one who had made use of the evangelics' doctrine so far, as to take a reasonable liberty to judge of the present times" (435).[15] The "one" puts forth arguments as close to deism as the fictionizing historian could at the furthest stretch of possibility imagine being said in the historical context. The appropriately nameless "one" speaks for the universal natural religion that belongs to everyone—as opposed to the private and willful positions that otherwise contend for supremacy.

Herbert as apologist?   Commentators have differed as to Herbert's attitude toward the subject of his longest book. The everhostile Sidney Lee calls *The Life and Reign* "an unmeasured eulogy of Henry VIII's statesmanship, and a laboured endeavor to condone the crimes of his private life."[16] Long before Lee, Horace Walpole had regretted that "a man who found it necessary to take up arms against Charles I should have palliated the enormities of Henry VIII, in comparison to whom, King Charles was an excellent prince."[17] Walpole was wrong on both counts. Lord Herbert never took up arms against his king; nor is the *Life and Reign* at its core a work of apologetics. That is only one of the voices in which Herbert speaks and not the fundamental one. The other and more powerful voice has been noticed by W. M. Merchant, who speaks of Herbert's "dislike of," his "detached irony towards the king."[18] Even Rossi, while undervaluing *The Life and Reign,* recognizes Herbert's basic lack of sympathy for Henry.[19]

What critics have not clearly stated is the link between the subject of this book and its author's work as a theorist of religion. That King Charles would want to look back at his potent predecessor is easy to understand. In separating England from the Roman Church, Henry had maintained most of that Church's doctrine and its hierarchical structuring of religious practice. On Henry Tudor, Charles could meditate with nostalgia, assaulted as he was by an increasingly powerful Puritan movement that accused him of leaning toward Rome. Herbert's interest in King Henry, though, was of a different order.

As A. F. Pollard writes in his classic biography of Henry VIII, "he is still the Great Erastian, the protagonist of laity against clergy." Pollard notes that the Henrician Reformation in England was "neither more nor less than a violent self-assertion of the laity against the immunities which the Church had herself enjoyed, and the restraints which she imposed upon others."[20] Such a champion of the laity would have great appeal to the author of the book propounding *The Layman's Religion.* In the *Life and Reign,* Herbert makes clear his belief that the early Protestant Reformers were aiming at just the sort of purifying of religion that he himself propounded. With Henry, however, it was a different story—and that difference is the subject of *The Life and Reign.*

With bitter irony, Herbert shows the steps by which Henry inflated himself into a tyrant no less menacing than Herbert deemed the pope. (Rossi aptly states that Herbert saw in both king and pope "enemies of liberty."[21]) In a crucial passage on Henry's persecution of Protestants and Catholics, Herbert writes: "The king continued yet his rigor to those that disputed either his authority, or articles; insomuch, that both the reformers and maintainers of the pope's authority suffered so frequently, that his enemies said, while he admitted neither side, he seemed to be of no religion. Howbeit, this was but calumny, for Henry stood firmly to his own reformation" (644). The Reformation that should free men to a universally valid religion has been subjected to one man's willfulness. Luther had already said of his contemporary, "Junker Heintz will be God and does whatever he lusts."[22]

Herbert's deeply ironic view of Henry distinguishes his book from either of the main lines of thought about the king. For the Catholics, of course, Henry Tudor was a beast; his break with Rome was motivated entirely by "lust and wickedness," wrote the sixteenth-century Catholic priest Nicholas Sanders. In the English Protestant tradition, Henry "was a great instrument in the hand of Providence"; even his "pride and passion" were necessary "to bring about, under the dread of his unrelenting temper, a change that a milder reign could not have compassed without great convulsions and much confusion."[23] These last remarks, from the pen of Bishop Gilbert Burnet (d. 1715), clearly state the view that Herbert rejects. Burnet's view is that of the apologist; Herbert's is not.

The portrait of Henry. If the idea of two simultaneous voices has helped to make clear Herbert's tone in *The Life and Reign,* another idea can help to define the shape Herbert gave his book. An artful biography is not a mass of facts; it is the plot of a career, a dramatic action with beginning, middle, and end. The image one needs is furnished by Herbert himself in the opening paragraph of the *Life.* "It is not easy to write that prince's history, of whom no one thing may constantly be affirmed. Changing of manners and condition alters the coherence of parts, which should give an uniform description. Nor is it probable that contradictories should agree to the same person: so that nothing can shake the credit of a narration more, than if it grow unlike itself; when yet it may be not the author, but the argument caused the variation. It is impossible to draw his picture well who hath several countenances" (109).

Herbert here plays upon a traditional definition of a hero as a man "equal to himself" in all phases of his life. Herbert's Henry is the opposite. Only the multiple exposures of successive and dissimilar portraits can be true to the man who was not true to himself.

For the young Henry Tudor, Herbert has nothing but praise. "Had his age answered his youth, or expectation, none of his predecessors could have exceeded him; but as his exquisite endowments of nature engaged him often to become a prey of these allurements and temptations, which are ordinarily incident unto them; so his courage was observed by little and little to receive into it some mixture of self-will and cruelty" (110). In the next sentence Herbert introduces the idea that underlies his multiple portraits of Henry. "Princes' actions are not always drawn from reason of state, but sometimes even from inclination and humour" (110). Herbert trusts rulers and statesmen who seek political ends through rational calculation. As he explains later on, "True reason of state consist[s] of such solid maxims, that it hath as little need of deceit, as a sure game at chess of a false draught" (168). But if the private and the irrational come to dominate a statesman's actions, he will become dangerously unpredictable. And that is what happened to Henry.

The agent of that transformation was Thomas Wolsey. "Of a quick and stirring wit, . . . he knew as well how to discourse with the king in matter of learning (the king being much addicted to the reading of Thomas Aquinas) as to comply with him in his delights." Soon "he began to tell the king, that he should sometimes follow his studies in school-divinity, and sometimes take his pleasure, and leave the care of public affairs to him." Moreover, "he omitted not to infuse fears and jealousies of all those whom he conceived the king might affect. Whereby he became so perfect a courtier, that he had soon attained the height of favor. For as princes have arts to govern kingdoms, courtiers have those by which they govern their princes" (139–40).

Henry ought to have known better. As Herbert writes, "Princes ought to take heed in whose hands they commit their extraordinary power, lest it hazzard their ordinary; it being the clue of the labyrinth of state, which ought not rashly to be put into another's hand" (267). Wolsey (now a cardinal) followed a policy of constant changefulness. "As the manner of the most subtle sort of favorites hath been not to study so much good as great actions, as hoping thereby to amuse and entertain their princes; so this cardinal, by the perpetual variation (he seemed to cause) in the affairs of Christendom, held not only the minds of the people in attention and suspense, but made his counsels more considerable to the king, than if he had pursued any one way" (219).

This "perpetual variation" maintained by "our cunning cardinal" (184) served his interests rather than the king's. Herbert writes that Wolsey "had his free scope and liberty to sway all things, under color of doing the king service. For, whatsoever he went about, that was his pretence; though (for the most part) in laboring to reform, he did nothing but innovate" (164). That is a serious charge in the Renaissance, when truth was always thought to lie in the original belief or practice, and innovation was deemed in principle harmful.

Herbert directs some keen barbs against Wolsey; thus he notes wryly that "the cardinal might be said to have in him so much of a good servant, as he willingly suffered none other to deceive his master" (172). But Herbert has a good measure of respect for Wolsey, whom he defends against some charges brought by earlier historians. In Herbert's view, Wolsey was a creature of rational calculation. "As he loved nobody, so his reason carried him" (461). He pursued a personal version of reason of state. "He was no great dissembler, for so qualified a person; as ordering his business for the most part so cautiously, as he got more by keeping his word than by breaking it" (462).

After recounting Wolsey's downfall—which Herbert attributes especially to the ill will borne him by Anne Boleyn, later Henry's second queen—Herbert modifies a judgment made by the historian Polydore Vergil. "If it be true (as Polydore observes) that no man ever did rise with fewer virtues, it is as true, that few that ever fell from so high a place had lesser crimes objected against them." Herbert adds that "during his favor with the king, all things succeeded better than afterwards" (462). And that for Herbert is the key point: the real damage Herbert attributes to the cardinal is that he served as a catalyst to bring out the worst in Henry Tudor.

The same unpredictability, the same preoccupation with jealousies and suspicious fears that had marked Wolsey's period of power now characterized Henry's regimen. Along with them came an ever-increasing cruelty that led him to shed the blood of wives and recalcitrant practitioners of religions that differed somewhat from his own. Even the proud structure of English law and government became a cloak for Henry's cruelty. Herbert writes, "I do not find him bloody, but where law, or at least pretext drawn from thence, did countenance his actions" (568). Herbert notes "with how high a hand the king did authorize his actions, while each part justified the other, and all his subjects' voices being comprehended in his parliament, no man could accuse him, who did not in some sort first condemn himself; . . . where he did ill, he made or found many complices" (585).

The later Henry has become a bit of a monster, whose doings must be softened with ironic formulations. Thus, after executing several wives, Henry has (Herbert reports in perfect deadpan) "some difficulty" in procuring another bride. "For as by a statute . . . it was declared death for any whom the king should marry, to conceal her incontinency in former time, so few durst hazard to venture into those bonds with a king, who had (as they thought) so much facility in dissolving them: therefore they stood off, as knowing in what a slippery estate they were, if the king, after his receiving them to bed, should, through any mistake, declare them no maids" (677). The delicate humor of that sentence both conceals and reveals a virtual reign of terror.

For all the king's vices, all his reliance on that extremity of law that is the height of injustice, Herbert cannot deny Henry a certain grandeur. "His most irregular actions represented such a type of greatness, as crooked lines drawn every way, which though not so compendious and direct as the straight, seem yet to have in them somewhat more of the infinite" (585).

The background of the portrait.   This final portrait of Henry Tudor emerges against a background (throughout Europe) defined by one concern: the idea of reformation. For in mocking counterpoint with Henry's massive self-will (his rule by "inclination and hu-mour"), *The Life and Reign* develops the theme of a simplifying return to the common sources of religion on which all Christians can in theory agree.

In the later sections of the book, which portray the king at his most irrational, Herbert frequently reports on attempts to call a grand council to reform Christianity. But the efforts are rendered unavailing by factious disputes. Princes of state and princes of the church, Herbert makes clear, have their own petty reasons—both reasons of state, and reasons of "inclination and humour"—to hold out each one for a "reformation of his own." Gradually, the reader of *The Life and Reign* comes to recognize an emblematic aptness in the seemingly awkward structure of the book. Henry's doings in England show in little what the corresponding year-by-year accounts of foreign affairs show on a larger stage: the disruption of significant reformation by princely self-will.

And the issue of reform lies (physically and thematically) at the center of *The Life and Reign*. In a lengthy speech, "one who had made use of the evangelics' doctrine so far as to take a reasonable liberty to judge of the present times" calls upon "laics and secular persons" like himself to establish a simplified code of belief. They must avoid the "particular reason" of any individual or faction but stick fast to the "common, authentic and universal truths" as these were "first written in the heart" (435–37). By so doing, the fictitious deist asserts, "we laics may so build upon those catholick and infallible grounds of religion, as whatsoever superstructures of faith be raised, those foundations yet may support them" (439). The upshot would be "an universal peace among Christians" (435)—the goal of any "one" of good will.

A deist peace—that, in Herbert's view, is what all the turmoil of early sixteenth-century Europe called for, and in fact what the early Reformers were really aiming at. It is what Henry ought to have had in mind when he set out "to make himself arbiter of Christendom." "Never prince went upon a truer maxim for this kingdom," Herbert ruefully observes. No more ironic background can be imagined for the emergence of Herbert's last portrait of that prince of "his own"—as opposed to a general—reformation.

The unquiet grave. In the final pages of the work, after he has narrated the king's death on 28 January 1547, Lord Herbert offers (as is usual in the book) a character sketch of the deceased. On this occasion he does so with evident reluctance.

And now if the reader (according to my manner in other great personages) do expect some character of this prince, I must affirm (as in the beginning) that the course of his life being commonly held various and diverse from itself, he will hardly suffer any, and that his history will be his best character and description. Howbeit, since others have so much defamed him, as will appear by the following objections, I shall strive to rectify their understandings who are impartial lovers of truth; without either presuming audaciously to condemn a prince, heretofore sovereign of our kingdom, or omitting the just freedom of an historian. (743–44)

The note of grudging defense will run through these final pages, not least the book's final sentence.

Herbert goes on to record the deeds that have provoked condemnation: Henry's "divorces and decapitations of his following wives, the dissolutions of the monasteries, and others his most branded actions," in all of which, Herbert notes, "he at least wanted not color and pretext to make them specious [i.e., outwardly acceptable] to the world; . . . outward esteem and reputation being the same to great persons which the skin is to the fruit, which though it be but a slight and delicate cover, yet without it the fruit will presently discolor and rot" (744). Herbert lists the vices alleged against Henry, especially willfulness and cruelty (745). Herbert again comments on Henry's genius at creating complicity in his misdeeds. "Things done by public vote, when they find not reason, make it" (746). (Such complicity is the very opposite of the true uniformity of belief and practice to which a deist aspired.) Herbert comments on another "vice, wherewith he was justly charged, being lust and wantonness; there is *little to answer,* more than it was rather a personal fault, than damageable to the public" (747).

The two final paragraphs weave all the threads of the book together.

With all his crimes, yet he was one of the most glorious princes of his time: insomuch, that not only the chief potentates of Christendom did court him, but his subjects in general did highly reverence him, as the many trials he put them to, sufficiently testify. Which [the reverence for him] yet expired so quickly, that it may be truly said, all his pomp died with him; his memory being now exposed to that obloquy, as his excusers will neither admit reason of state to cover anywhere, or necessity to excuse his actions. . . .

.   .   .

But what this prince was, and whether, and how far forth excusable in point of state, conscience, or honor, a diligent observation of his actions, together with a conjuncture of the times, will (I conceive) better declare to the judicious reader, than any factious relation on what side whatsoever. To conclude: I wish I could leave Henry VIII in his grave. (747–48)

The note of weariness here is evident. Insofar as he is defensible, Henry has been defended, though to little avail: the attacks continue. Herbert regrets having to enter a debate that factious and self-interested persons have not allowed to die out in a merciful silence. That remarkable final sentence has stirred critics to commentary. Arthur Slavin remarks that Herbert "saw in Henry enough vice to make him wish that he could leave the king in his grave."[24] Judith Anderson rightly notes the inverted echo here of the concluding words of Bacon's life of Henry VII: "he dwelleth more richly dead, in the monuments of his tomb, than he did alive in Richmond or any of his palaces. I could wish he did the like in this monument of his fame."[25] Anderson's interpretation of Herbert's allusion here is no more satisfying than Slavin's reading of the passage. She sees "I wish I could leave [him] in his grave" as Herbert's "final negation of art" in contrast with the Baconian "affirmation of art."[26] But surely the closing words of Herbert's book suggest, first of all, his exasperation with the continuing debate over Henry's deserts—a debate maintained by biased and self-serving parties. The last sentence also suggests Herbert's weary knowledge that the obstructive self-will embodied in Henry Tudor—in his wrangling Thomism no less than in his bloody persecutions—had not been laid to rest in the century since that monarch's death.

Chapter Five
Herbert's Early Poems

Judgments of Lord Herbert's poetic gift have varied widely. In his Clarendon edition of 1923, G. C. Moore Smith wrote: "I am inclined to claim that in poetic feeling and art Edward Herbert soars above his brother George."[1] This is a large claim, even when one has allowed for the fact that George Herbert's reputation was not then what it is today.

The other modern editor of Lord Herbert's verse, Churton Collins, noted in 1881 that in his esteem for Herbert's poems he "stood alone. [Herbert's] biographers and critics are unanimous in ignoring or condemning them."[2] In 1900 Leslie Stephen called Herbert "a third-rate poet."[3] For Rossi, Herbert is an occasional poet, who composed only when he felt "socially obliged" to do so. Rossi deems Herbert's verses cold—the product of intellectual diversion, not of that inner need for expressing one's soul that Rossi considers the source of true poetry.[4]

The renewal of interest early this century in the metaphysical poets led some critics to reread Herbert's poems in light of T. S. Eliot's new characterization of Donne. (Churton Collins had already noted that Herbert was the first of Donne's English disciples.) Discussions soon appeared concerned with whether Lord Herbert's sensibility united feeling and thought as the master's was said to. R. G. Howarth answered in the affirmative. Herbert "feels his thought to a degree which only Donne could exceed, and it is this basis of deep feeling which imparts such sustained harmony and beauty of form to the finest of his poems."[5] In *The School of Donne*, however, A. Alvarez contended that Herbert "does not 'feel his thoughts'; he abstracts his feelings. He is a perfect example not of the unified but of the dialectical sensibility."[6] Similarly, Patrick Cruttwell in *The Shakespearean Moment* explicitly treated Herbert as a test case of the dissolution of the unified sensibility effected by rationalist skepticism. For Cruttwell, Herbert "was a metaphysical only on the surface, only (to put it crudely) because his friends were." While Cruttwell admitted that Herbert's poems always show intelligence, he claimed that they rarely show much else. "Except in rare flashes, his thinking is terribly non-incandescent."[7]

In some measure, Robert Ellrodt escapes from this issueless debate on the unity of Herbert's sensibility. The long chapter on Herbert in the Frenchman's thesis stands as the finest published treatment of Herbert's verse. Ellrodt rightly distinguishes the elements of preciosity and Platonism in Herbert's poetry from the metaphysical and Christian elements in Donne. But Ellrodt's advance over his predecessors proves halfhearted. Constrained by the Sartrean psychology that provides the analytic framework for his study, he attributes the distinctive features of Herbert's poetry to the author's hidden psychological penchants. Pursuing what he calls the secret logic of authors' individual orientations, Ellrodt ignores the philosophical and aesthetic choices that are more likely to have governed so diplomatic a writer as Herbert.[8]

Herbert's poems will not yield their riches to readers intent on seeing them as successful (or unsuccessful) ventures to write like John Donne. Even those early poems that most clearly ape Donne's style are built upon thematic concerns that are distinctively Herbertian. And the best poems of Herbert's maturity combine what he learned from Donne with what he learned from Continental masters like the Italian Marino into a voice that is his alone.

Two poems in Donne's Style

"The State progress of Ill." Edward Herbert's earliest datable English poem was written in August 1608 at the Montmorency estate at Merlou, as a note appended to the work specifies. In its argument, "The State progress of Ill" shows the influence of the daring political speculation that Herbert encountered on his first visit to France. But in form, the poem's debts are to Donne. Herbert writes in the same nonendstopped couplets made difficult by rough meter and even rougher sense that Donne had used in his satires of the 1590s. And the very title of Herbert's poem plays on another of Donne's satirical poems, "The Progress of the Soul" (1601). There Donne had used the metempsychosis of a soul to tie together a harsh overview of human evil. Part of Donne's concern was political; he attacked the dog-eat-dog character of social relations. Presenting the kingdom of the sea as an analogue of human society, Donne wrote:

> Fish chaseth fish, and all,
> Flyer and follower, in this whirlpool fall;
> O might not states of more equality
> Consist? and is it of necessity
> That thousand guiltless smalls, to make one great, must die?[9]

The play on different senses of *states*—both statuses, conditions; and political entities, nations—probably suggested Herbert's title. And that title adumbrates the much sharper political focus of Herbert's poem: not progress but state progress. Tracing the "progression" of evil, Herbert undertakes a study of the political bonds by which men are held in subjection. All of history seems a triumphant march of the principle of iniquitous domination: a "progress" like that of a sovereign traveling through his realm.

Unlike Donne's satires, Herbert's poem offers a critique of government in itself, not of this or that defective practice. And the theoretical rigor of Herbert's poem has a specific source in a mid-sixteenth-century book: Étienne de la Boétie's *Discourse on Voluntary Servitude*. A favorite of militant French Protestants in Herbert's time, this book would be reprinted by progressives or revolutionaries at every major crisis of French history, including the Revolution and the Nazi occupation. La Boétie writes with astonishment of the fact that men allow themselves to be ruled by a king. "The people cut their own throat. Having the choice of being serf or free, they abandon freedom and assume the yoke; they consent to their own evil—rather, they pursue it."[10]

La Boétie's point, that men connive in, indeed come to crave, their own subjection, is well captured by the conclusion of Herbert's poem: "freeborn man" has been "subdued / By his own choice" and now serves monarchy.

> then why wonder men
> Their rule of horses?
> The World, as in the ark of *Noah*, rests,
> Composed as then, few Men, and many Beasts.

In the body of the poem, Herbert argues that political society is in its very nature evil, though perhaps necessary:

> I do see
> Some Ill required, that one poison might free

> The other; so states, to their Greatness, find
> No faults required but their own, and bind
> The rest.
>
> (ll. 9–13)

Evil has prospered so greatly that men can no more live as well without kings as with them than they could be without original sin and yet be saved (ll. 69–72); of course, Herbert wants his reader to interject that without original sin there would be no need for men to be saved in the first place. Herbert goes on to explain the ordering of society that maintains subjection. By a kind of optical illusion, men are made to believe that the exalted nobility are superior to other folk (ll. 81–102). And "sugared divines" preach that people should seek their kingdom in the next world, that "the greatest rule here / Is for to rule ourselves" (ll. 106–7). And the system includes a set of mechanisms to entangle those "whose harder minds Religion / Cannot invade, nor turn from thinking on / A present greatness."

> that Combined curse of Law,
> Of officers, and neighbors' spite, doth draw
> Within such whirlpools, that till they be drowned,
> They n'ere get out, but only swim them round.
>
> (ll. 111–16)

The poem is a notable performance in which Herbert imbues the form of Donnean satire with a distinctive theoretical polemic derived from a Continental text.

The elegy for Prince Henry. Four years later, Herbert wrote another poem in Donne's "strong lines," an elegy for young Prince Henry, who died in November 1612. The prince had been a great favorite of militant Protestants, who expected much from him. They were fond of comparing him to King Henry VIII and predicted that the prince would complete the Reformation of the English Church begun by his royal namesake.[11]

The "Elegy for the Prince" (published 1613) elicited the earliest recorded comment on Herbert's verse. Ben Jonson told Drummond of Hawthornden "that Donne said he wrote [his] Epitaph on Prince Henry . . . to match Sir Edward Herbert in obscureness."[12] The remark is more a jest than a piece of criticism, although it is not clear whose leg is being pulled.

Herbert's "Elegy" is based on an idea he would have known from Donne's two *Anniversaries* (1612). Each poet treats the deceased as the soul of the world, which (deprived of its soul) is now in effect dead. But where Donne's two poems celebrate a young girl of good family, Herbert memorializes a prince. Donne's hyperbolic proposition (deceased = soul of the world) leads him into obscure realms of Christianized Platonic theory of knowledge. Herbert, instead, adapts Donne's proposition to a specifically political subject. And he does so by way of a bit of Platonic theory that was a commonplace of political thinking in the period. Prince Henry was, or was destined to be, a sovereign. And it was generally held that the sovereign is the soul of the state, while the subjects form its body. Without their ruler the people (the body politic) are helpless. These points are made very clearly in Edward Forset's *Comparative discourse of the bodies natural and politique* (1606).

Critics have disparaged Herbert's "Elegy" for not relating the public issue to the poet's interior life, as Donne would do in his.[13] But that is to miss the point of Herbert's rhetoric. It is not his voice that the "Elegy" offers us. The poem abounds in first-person-plural forms, and its "obscureness" is much dissipated once the reader figures out why. The "we" that speaks represents the embodied, but now soulless, voice of the British people. To evoke that voice, Herbert was confronted with a technical problem that might faze an author of science fiction. How would a zombie talk? He might well speak largely in questions, many of these negative in grammatical form. His gestures of self-assertion would be indirect, moving by fits and starts. But he would keep saying the pronoun that embodies all the self he has left. And this is just the voice Herbert creates in the "Elegy." "Must he be ever dead? Cannot we add / Another life unto that Prince that had / Our souls laid up in him?" (ll. 1–3).

The poem moves toward the most limited of affirmations.

> We and posterity
> Shall celebrate his name, and virtuous grow,
> Only in memory that he was so;
> And on those terms we may seem yet to live,
> Because he lived once, though we shall strive
> To sigh away this seeming life so fast,
> As if with us 'twere not already past.

> We then are dead, for what doth now remain
> To please us more, or what can we call pain,
> Now we have lost him?
>
> (ll. 44–52)

Again, as with "The State progress of Ill," Herbert has taken Donnean themes and forms and made them carriers of his more rigorously political point of view. It may seem surprising to find Herbert in the "Elegy" presenting with apparent approval that total dependence of subject upon sovereign condemned in the earlier poem. But it would be more accurate to see the two works as photographic negatives of one another, each bearing the indubitable mark of Herbert's distinctive intelligence. The two poems embody the two sides of the issue raised by Edward Forset when he notes that "sacred and unsearchable Majesty" represents as great an *Arcanum* in policy [politics] as the soul can be in nature."[14] A good lawyerly orator, Herbert makes the case for or against, as he finds himself called upon to do.

The Influence of Marino

A number of early poems show that Herbert had studied the verse of an Italian contemporary of Donne's, Giambattista Marino. Perhaps the most influential poet in Western Europe in the first quarter of the seventeenth century, Marino shared with Donne a penchant for verbal wit. But the Italian's poems are far less argumentative and discursive. He delights in weaving an elaborate web of images— the more surprising the better—to capture the fetching poses of his beloved lady. An inspired celebrator of the trivial, Marino may find the basis of a poem "in meditating on how [the lady] washes her feet, sews, plays the viol, rolls dice, or plays tennis."[15]

Herbert's early poem "A Vision," in part based on one of Marino's,[16] describes a lady combing her hair. The preciosity of this poem has won it few admirers.

> Within an *open curled Sea of Gold*
> A *Bark of Ivory*, one day, I saw,
> Which striking with his *Oars* did seem to draw
> Towards a fair *Coast*, which I then did behold.

Herbert comes much closer to the Italian master in another poem on the same theme, "Upon Combing her Hair." Here Herbert

captures the elegant verbal music in which Marino so often evokes
the lady in poems at once worshipful and playful. A free variation
on a familiar Marinesque subject, it is one of Herbert's finest poems.
Ellrodt enlists the names of Spenser and Shelley in praising the
splendid opening stanza.[17]

> Breaking from under that thy cloudy vail,
> Open and shine yet more, shine out more clear
> Thou glorious golden-beam-darting hair,
> Even till my wonderstrucken Senses fail.

The poem proceeds to make a little etymological joke, comparing
the lady's flowing hair to a comet, a word that comes from the
Greek for "long-haired star."

> Shoot out in light, and shine those Rays on far,
> Thou much more fair than is the Queen of love,
> When she doth comb her in her Sphere above,
> And from a planet turns a Blazing-Star.
>
> (st. 2)

The lady in combing separates the strands of her hair, the poet
asserts, lest their combined glory overwhelm the observer's senses.
When her hairs are spread, they show her as one whom "Heaven's
beams did crown" (20). The poem concludes:

> But stay, methinks, new Beauties do arise,
> While she withdraws these Glories which were spread.
> Wonder of Beauties, set thy radiant head,
> And strike out day from thy yet fairer eyes.
>
> (st. 7)

Another favorite subject of Marino's is the *bacio,* or kiss. In many
poems the Italian evokes the different kinds of kisses, and Herbert
tries his hand at this fashionable subject in "Kissing."

> Give me the billing-Kiss, that of the dove,
> A Kiss of love;
> ....
> The twaching smacking Kiss, and when you cease
> A Kiss of Peace;

> The Music-Kiss, crotchet and quaver time,
> The Kiss of Rime.
>
> (ll. 3–4, 11–14)

The celebratory music of these Marinesque poems might seem to have little connection with the rugged critical satires of Herbert's Donnean style. But it would not do to call these Italianate ventures mere court trifles. Like his prose, Herbert's mature poems will speak (as it were) in two simultaneous voices; one can call them the Marinesque and the Donnean. In his best later poems, the blandly laudatory surface will veil the sharp insinuations of the philosopher-poet.

Other Early Poems

Four sonnets. Some other early poems show additional influences on Herbert's work. Particularly notable are four sonnets: "To her Face," "To her Body," "To her Mind," and an untitled conclusion that Moore Smith calls "Love's End." Here one finds Herbert taking up the themes of the Elizabethan sonnet sequence in a couple of pages. The virtuosic effect is rather like one of those early twentieth-century Viennese pieces of music that runs through the form of a classical symphony in less than five minutes.

Herbert's sequence moves from infatuation at first glance to the ultimate rejection that the lover suffers. Each poem makes evident the speaker's veritable idolatry of the lady. Thus the first poem begins and ends with that "Fatal . . . Face."

> Fatal aspect! that hast an Influence
> More powerful far than those Immortal Fires
> That but incline the Will and move the Sense,
> Which thou alone constrain'st, kindling Desires
> Of such an holy force, as more inspires
> The Soul with Knowledge, than Experience
> Or Revelation can do with all
> Their borrowed helps: Sacred Astonishment
> Sits on thy Brow, threat'ning a sudden fall
> To all those Thoughts that are not lowly sent,
> In wonder and amaze, dazzling that Eye
> Which on those Mysteries doth rudely gaze,
> Vowed only unto Love's Divinity:
> Sure *Adam* sinned not in that spotless Face.

The lady's perfection cannot be put into words any more than the divinity's can. So "To her Mind" builds to a line of breathless silence. "Then pardon me . . . / . . . that want, for what I see, / Description, if here amazed I cease /Thus———— "(ll. 8–11). (This is one of those metrical ploys that the younger brother George Herbert may well have picked up from his elder brother's work. Both poets are also remarkable for the variety of stanza forms they employ; thus, the four sonnets under discussion use three different rhyme schemes.[18]) At this point the poem changes tone, ending with a thrust at the lady. "Yet grant one Question, and no more, craved under / Thy gracious leave, how, if thou would'st express / Thy self to us, thou should'st be still a wonder?" (ll. 12–14).

The beloved's refusal to make known her feelings for him ("express / Thy self to us"—the language also for a deity's communicating its nature to a mortal, here used tauntingly) is seen as a strategic move on her part. By it she maintains her air of mystery and her power over the speaker.

The sequence ends with the speaker attempting to undo his infatuation. "There only rests but to unpaint / Her form in my mind, that so dispossest / It be a Temple, but without a Saint." The lover undertakes a Reformation of his mind, the poet hinting that blind devotion may be unnatural and disabling in love as well as in religion.

"Ditty."   Herbert was a musician of some skill. His lute book (in the Fitzwilliam Museum, Cambridge University) includes not only his own compositions; it is the unique source for pieces by composers as important as John Dowland.[19] A number of Herbert's poems were certainly meant to be sung, including one entitled "Ditty." The speaker urges a lady not to refuse his love, thinking she can later accept.

> If you refuse me once, and think again,
> I will complain,
> You are deceived: Love is no work of Art,
> It must be got and born,
> Not made and worn,
> Or such wherein you have no part.
> . . . .
> Or do you think it is too soon to yield,
> And quit the Field?
> You are deceived, they yield who first intreat;

> Once one may crave for love,
> Bur more would prove
> This heart too little, that too great.
>
> (st. 1, 3)

The poem looks back to the courtly lyrics of Thomas Wyatt as it deftly balances tough self-regard and proffered affection in a strategic game of amatory one-upmanship. Like Wyatt, Herbert weaves his argument through a pattern of long and short lines, mixing short, simple words to achieve richly sonorous (and singable) rhymes. The second half of the poem (st. 4–6) evokes the possibilities of love in language closer to Donne's.

> Then give me so much love, that we may move
> Like stars of love,
> And glad and happy times to Lovers bring;
> While glorious in one sphere
> We still appear,
> And keep an everlasting Spring.
>
> (st. 6)

"Elegy over a Tomb." It is appropriate to end this chapter by looking at another of Herbert's memorial poems, the lovely "Elegy over a Tomb" (1617) for an unknown lady. This poem shows the very high level of poetic craftsmanship that Herbert had attained by the time he began his ambassadorial years. The "Elegy" also finds Herbert subtly bringing some of his philosophical concerns into an occasional poem.

The elegy is built on the supposition that the lady must have restored her "beauties" to the world. Otherwise, the poet argues, all beauty would have been extinguished.

> Doth the Sun now his light with yours renew?
> Have Waves the curling of your hair?
> Did you restore unto the Sky and Air,
> The red, and white, and blue?
> Have you vouchsafed to flowers since your death
> That sweetest breath?
>
> Had not Heav'n's Lights else in their houses slept,
> Or to some private life retir'd?
> Must not the Sky and Air have else conspir'd,

And in their Regions wept?
Must not each flower else the earth could breed
Have been a weed?

But thus enrich'd may we not yield some cause
Why they themselves lament no more?
That must have changed the course they held before,
And broke their proper Laws,
Had not your beauties giv'n this second birth
To Heaven and Earth?

(st. 3–5)

Wittily the poet reverses the usual metaphors for female beauty:
rather than her hair being sunlike, the sun is like her hair. Herbert
also inverts a standard topic of memorial poetry. If in his earlier
elegy the prince's death has disvalued the world, here a death revalues
the world, gives it a "second birth."

Few readers, though, will condemn the "Elegy over a Tomb" as
an empty pursuit of uncommon ways of treating a familiar subject.
Rather, the poem presents a polite fiction (the world's "second
birth") to account for the absence of change in the world. What
Ruskin called the "pathetic fallacy" leads the speaker to expect
nature to share his grief. And he develops a little myth to account
for the observed absence of change.

What has changed, of course, is his way of looking at the world.
He now sees it as throughout reflecting the lady's glories: she has
become the Creator of his world. Or he tries to view her as such.
For the final stanza makes clear that even he cannot accept his little
myth.

Tell us, for Oracles must still ascend,
For those that crave them at your tomb:
Tell us, where are those beauties now become
And what they now intend:
Tell us, alas, that cannot tell our grief
Or hope relief.

(st. 6)

The poem emerges as a careful look at human fabulation—at the
need to see nature transfigured in the image of desire. The speaker

has almost started a religion out of nothing. Not without significance is the fact that the "Elegy" is contemporary with Herbert's first work on *De Veritate*.

Chapter Six
Herbert's Later Poems
The Poems in Praise of Black Beauty

Herbert's mature verse style combined Donne's philosophical imagery with Marino's celebratory descriptions of female beauty into poems quite different from either predecessor's. A good example of Herbert at the top of his form is the sequence of poems in praise of a black-haired lady (ca. 1621, according to Moore Smith).

The first poem is addressed to Diana Cecil, "the greatest beauty of her day and a great heiress."[1] The six poems in praise of black beauty can be read as a transcript of a failed love affair. But their true strength and interest emerge only if they are read as poems that claim their place in a long tradition of celebrating darkness.

Praisers of blackness. The tradition had never been more vigorously alive than in the early seventeenth century. Shakespeare's so-called Dark Lady furnishes the best-known example in English literature. In Continental literature, the most celebrated instance was the black lady praised by Marino in a sonnet published in 1614 and soon famous all over Europe. It began: "Black you are, but beautiful, o pretty monster of love among nature's beauties."[2] Marino's opening words would have recalled the Song of Songs 1:5ff. "I am black, but comely. . . ." And readers of classical literature would have remembered one of the poems in the *Greek Anthology*: "Looking on her beauty, I melt like wax before the fire. And if she is dusky [*melaina*], what is that to me? So are the coals, but when we light them, they shine as bright as roses."[3]

Herbert's poems differ, though, from any of these earlier verse panegyrics on dark beauty. Marino, like the celebrated Old Testament poet he echoes, assumes that black itself is not supposed to give delight. The lady is black—but, nonetheless, beautiful. Herbert's poem attributes his lady's beauty to the very power and purity of her blackness. And in so doing, Herbert draws upon another strand of the tradition: the paradoxical praise of blackness.

Such praise is literally paradoxical—it goes against the received opinion. Black was normally associated with the lowly and material, while white was linked with the spiritual and divine, as by Ficino.[4] A Jacobean writer on heraldry said that "whatsoever was holden reproachful or dishonorable, was noted with black." But the early seventeenth century being an age greatly given to paradox, another English writer on heraldry can be found according the precedence to black over white. "The color of black is the most ancient of all colors, for in the beginning there was darkness over the face of the earth."[5] He has in mind the Creation in Genesis, which begins with "Let there be light"; hence Donne could refer to darkness as "light's elder brother."[6] If a Greek source was wanted to supplement the Hebrew, one could refer to the mystical hymns attributed to Orpheus, in which Night is called "parent Goddess . . . / From whom at first both Gods and men arose."[7] And a writer in Herbert's day did not have to go directly to the ancient texts for all these references; he could pick up Caspar Dornau's enormous anthology of paradoxical panegyrics (1619), which touches all the classical bases in its section in praise of shadow and night.[8]

The tradition has yet another strand relevant to Herbert's sequence. Praise of blackness need not be mock-serious. Few authors are less so than the so-called Dionysius the Areopagite, author of *The Mystical Theology*. Yet he is much given to praising "the Divine darkness," "which in its deepest darkness shines above the most super-brilliant."[9] This was a familiar notion to mystical and contemplative authors, not least in the early seventeenth century. The truly transcendent was thought to surpass any distinction that could be imagined in the earthly realm between darkness and light. The absolute cannot be held within any human concept, but darkness seems the most apt image, in that darkness points to that very inaccessibility. To put the matter another way, the absolute shines so brightly that it appears as darkness to our insufficient powers of earthly perception.

This may seem quite a freight of tradition for six short poems to bear. But the reader must keep it in mind in order to follow the wonderfully nimble effects that Herbert has wrought in his black sequence.

Herbert's verse sequence. The opening poem, "To Mistress Diana Cecil," introduces the main theme of the sequence: the lady's uncommon (because dark) beauty, the poet's knowledge of which should gain him preference over other admirers.

> *Diana Cecil,* that rare beauty thou dost show
> Is not of Milk, or Snow,
> Or such as pale and whitely things do owe.
> But an illustrious Oriental Bright,
> Like to the Diamonds refracted light,
> Or early Morning breaking from the Night.
>
>   (st. 1)

The second stanza deals with her hair and eyes (the subjects of the next two poems in the sequence).

> Nor is thy hair and eyes made of that ruddy beam,
> Or golden-sanded stream,
> Which we find still the vulgar Poets' theme,
> But reverend black, and such as you would say,
> Light did but serve it, and did shew the way,
> By which at first night did precede the day.
>
>   (st. 2)

Herbert alludes here to the priority of darkness over light in the Old Testament and the Orphic hymns. The lady's distinctive beauty guides the poet-speaker toward an understanding of the mysteries of Creation. It also enables him as a creator in verse to avoid the hackneyed imagery of "the vulgar Poets."

In the third stanza, the poet speaks more abstractly of the lady's beauty. Its symmetry and proportion are said to manifest an indefinable perfection. (This stanza corresponds to the fourth and fifth poems of the sequence, which deal with black in itself.) In the fourth and final stanza, the speaker returns to the lady (as he will in the sixth and final poem of the sequence). Surpassing human wit, she is to be admired, though not understood. The poem's final lines, like the couplet of a Shakespearean sonnet, turn from description to prescription. Still addressing the lady, whom he has just called "wonder of all thy Sex!," the speaker warns this ideal figure not to lower herself to unworthy admirers. "Only be not with common praises wooed / Since admiration were no longer good, / When men might hope more than they understood" (ll. 22–24).

The next poem, "To her Eyes," explains that if her eyes "seem dark, / It is because your beams are deep, / And with your soul united keep" (ll. 1–3). And as the black eyes "joined are / Unto the Soul" (ll. 12–13), the lady's soul in turn is linked to the Creator, who

> By you doth best declare
> How he at first being hid
> Within the veil of an eternal night,
> Did frame for us a second light,
> And after bid
> It serve for ordinary sight.
>
> (ll. 17–22)

The poem's third and concluding stanza introduces a new image to make evident "What power it is that doth look out / Through that your black" (ll. 25–26). To look at the sun one would do well to use "grey, or hazel Glass." The lady far surpasses the sun; her rays can pass through pure black (which would filter out the first, or ordinary, light). And that is what one sees in her eyes: "beams which pass / Through black, cannot but be divine" (ll. 32–33). The claim of divinity with which the poem ends comes, appropriately, in the thirty-third line, a number associated with the life of Christ (none of Herbert's other English poems is of this length).

In the next poem, the speaker raises his sight a bit, his progression from eye to hair corresponding to the process described in the lovely opening stanza of "To her Hair."

> Black beamy hairs, which so seem to arise
> From the extraction of those eyes,
> That into you she destin-like doth spin
> The beams she spares, what time her soul retires,
> And by those hallowed fires,
> Keeps house all night within.

Herbert here plays upon a traditional theory of vision, according to which the eye sends out rays that enable it to see.[10] The poet calls the lady's eye-beams "threads of life," "fatal rays" (ll. 8–9) which "do crown those temples, where Love's wonders wrought / We afterwards see brought / To vulgar light and praise" (ll. 10–12). Some of these rays are retained, the poet imagines, transformed into hairs that crown the "temples" of her head.

The poet seeks to learn "the causes why we are grown blind" (l. 14) from looking at the lady. Is it, he asks, that black, as boundary

(and, one might say, container) of all the other colors, partakes of
the infinite, and as such is beyond the ken of mortal senses (st. 4)?

> Or is it, that the center of our sight
> Being veiled in its proper night
> Discerns your blackness by some other sense,
> Than that by which it doth pied colors see,
> Which only therefore be
> Known by their difference?
>
> (st. 5)

Here the poet distinguishes between ordinary ("pied") colors,
which merge into one another by degrees, and black, which is
absolutely itself and is recognized "by some other sense"—a part
of the mind akin to its glorious essence.

The lady's hair can teach its admirers to "know / That shining
light in darkness" (ll. 33–34) which they fail to see, being "upward
blind / With the Sun beams below" (ll. 35–36). For there are two
kinds of light, and a vision corresponding to each: common white
light, and secret black light. One's receptiveness to the former blinds
one to the superior brilliance of blackness—the topic to which
Herbert turns in the two succeeding poems.

In the "Sonnet of Black Beauty," the poet celebrates "black beauty,
which above that common light" (l. 1)

> Art neither changed with day, nor hid with night;
> When all these colors which the world call bright,
> And which old Poetry doth so pursue,
>
> Are with the night so perished and gone,
> That of their being there remains no mark,
> Thou still abidest so entirely one,
> That we may know thy blackness is a spark
> Of light inaccessible, and alone
> Our darkness which can make us think it dark.
>
> (ll. 6–14)

The lady has disappeared from the argument as the poet ascends
Platonically from an individual dark lady to Black Beauty as an
Idea. And the succeeding poem moves a bit further into the abstract.
The term *Beauty* drops away (as if redundant) in "Another Sonnet

to Black it self." Here black becomes the generative power of all
realms of nature.

> Thou Black, wherein all colors are composed,
> And unto which they all at last return,
> Thou color of the Sun where it doth burn,
> And shadow, where it cools, in thee is closed
> Whatever nature can, or hath disposed
> In any other Hue: from thee do rise
> Those tempers and complexions, which disclosed,
> As parts of thee, do work as mysteries,
> Of that thy hidden power; when thou dost reign
> The characters of fate shine in the Skies,
> And tell us what the Heavens do ordain,
> But when Earth's common light shines to our eyes,
> Thou so retir'st thy self, that thy disdain
> All revelation unto Man denies.

To black is attributed fire and shadow and everything between:
all human temperaments and complexions (both words refer to the
mixture of fluid humors thought to determine personality) and all
predictive signs in the heavens. The gorgeously expansive language
of the poem carries the reader outward to a large vision of nature;
this sonnet (like its predecessor) is all one sentence, as if to show
the unifying power of black. But the final three lines of the poem
bring the reader back to earth, at least on second reading. At first,
one may only register the lines as saying that in daylight one is
without the vision of darkness that is the poem's subject. But such
words as *disdain* and *denies* call up a personal reading. Behind the
elaborate cosmological imagery one intuits the lady, proud in her
embodiment of black itself, retiring in disdain from the speaker.
Behind the abstract "Hue" one recognizes the specific "you." The
poem's seeming impersonality evaporates. As with a Shakespearean
sonnet, every argumentative gesture or imagistic touch bears on the
speaker's relationship with the beloved, whatever its seeming gen-
erality of reference.

The final poem of the sequence, "The first Meeting," recounts
the steps the speaker has passed through in his relations with the
lady. At first terrified by the prodigious "blaze / Light'ning and
sparkling from [her] eyes" (ll. 7–8), he vanquished his fears when
he came to know her gentleness (st. 2). He even enjoyed a kiss in

which—as the Platonic treatises on love prescribed—the two exchanged souls (st. 4).

> But as those bodies which dispense
> Their beams, in parting hence
> Those beams do recollect,
> Until they in themselves resumed have
> The forms they gave,
> So when your gracious aspect
> From me was turned once away,
> Neither could I thy soul retain,
> Nor you gave mine leave to remain,
> To make with you a longer stay,
> Or suffered ought else to appear
> But your hair, night's hemisphere.
>
> (st. 5)

Using such words as *aspect* (a technical term in astronomy) and
hemisphere, the poet describes the lady's withdrawal as if it were a
planetary movement—slow, fated, predictable. No more distinc-
tions are made between different kinds of light, different kinds of
vision. In the blackness of the lady's hair one can now sense the
speaker's desolation.

In the poem's final stanza, he puts the best face he can on his
abandonment, comparing himself to a lodestone that has been
magnetized.

> So though I be from you retired,
> The power you gave yet still abides,
> And my soul ever so guides,
> By your magnetic touch inspired,
> That all it moves, or is inclined,
> Comes from the motions of your mind.
>
> (ll. 67–72)

That last phrase again calls to mind the long slow rhythm of the
spheres. But it also suggests the movement—changefulness, fick-
leness—that has victimized the poet-speaker.

As the preceding analysis has sought to show, the sequence balances a freight of sometimes esoteric learning against a familiar tale
of longing and loss. The tendency of readers will be to get so involved

in annotating the learning as to miss the ironic qualifications it takes on from the emerging story. For all his efforts at idealizing the lady, the speaker remains very much under her domination. His idealizing gestures emerge (like those of Shakespeare in his sonnets) in part as a process of self-deception. Then, too, those gestures come to seem an effort to achieve some power over her by proclaiming himself a priestlike knower of her mysteries.

The sequence concludes with a change of imagery: from the images of light that have predominated throughout to that of the magnet. Probably Herbert had in mind Plato's *Ion,* a prime text in Renaissance poetic theory. There Plato compared the poetic gift to a magnetic charge that passes from poet to reader. When in line 68 of "The first Meeting" Herbert asserts that "the power you gave yet still abides," he may well have in mind the poetic power that his sequence manifests. That power may be the happy precipitate of the power game of amatory one-upmanship in which he and the lady have been engaged. In that game, Platonic idealizing is only another move.

Poems on Other Colors

Brown and white. Black is not the only color Herbert praises in his verse. In "The Brown Beauty" he celebrates a woman he calls "Phaie," whose color perfectly blends "the two contraries of Black and White" (l. 1). The poet denigrates both extremes in favor of the brown mean.

> Therefore as it presents not to the view
> That whitely raw and unconcocted hue,
> Which Beauty Northern Nations think the true;
> So neither hath it that adust [burned] aspect,
> The *Moor* and *Indian* so much affect,
> That for it they all others do reject.
>
> (st. 2)

In the lady's brown, both black and white find their perfection. "Thus while the White well shadowed doth appear / And black doth through his luster grow so clear, / That each in other equal part doth bear" (ll. 13–15).

In another poem, Herbert lauds the golden hue of "The Sunburned Exotique Beauty." And Herbert even manages to write in commendation of the white skin praised in countless love poems, although he does so in a roundabout way. In two poems each entitled "The Green-Sickness Beauty," he addresses a young woman afflicted with "chlorosis, a variety of iron deficiency anemia" that was "popularly known as the green-sickness or the virgin's disease."[11] The first and more beautiful of the poems begins:

> Though the pale white within your cheeks composed,
> And doubtful light unto your eye confined,
> Though your short breath not from it self unloosed,
> And careless motions of your equal mind,
> Argue, your beauties are not all disclosed.
>
> (st. 1)

The wonderfully hesitant rhythm here evokes the combination of eagerness and timidity with which the girl looks toward adulthood. The girl's innocence (her "equal mind") makes the carelessness of her "motions" without danger to anyone. Escaped for a moment from the strategic games of love, Herbert can toy with the notion that the girl's sedate pallor is preferable to the blazing colors of adult experience.

> So in your green and flourishing estate
> A beauty is discerned more worthy love,
> Than that which further doth it self dilate . . .
>
> (ll. 11–13)
> ....
> Thus though your eyes dart not that piercing blaze,
> Which doth in busy Lovers' looks appear,
> It is, because you do not need to gaze,
> On other object than your proper sphere,
> Nor wander further than to run that maze.
>
> (st. 4)

But into his flattering portrayal of the girl's self-sufficiency Herbert insinuates a hint of how short-lived it must be, of how sterile her singleness would become if maintained beyond its due moment. A green fruit, she will yet ripen, and "love for his right will call" (l. 31).

   Color and the colorable.   Herbert's fondness for writing panegyrics on a given color of skin or hair or eye reveals something of his poetic orientation. It would be absurd to speak of insincerity on his part in his praise of different and contrary colors in different poems. But critics have tended to go to the other extreme; they look for intrinsic philosophical significance in one or another of the colors. Of course Herbert makes such arguments, but they cancel one another out. His true interest in the matter may well be thought to lie elsewhere: not in this or that color, but in the idea of color and the colorable.

These terms, it must be remembered, have (and had in the Renaissance) several senses. As poet, Herbert is adept at applying to a topic the tropes and schemes of language that are still called the "colors of rhetoric."[12] But color had another sense: the one-sided or biased presentation of a case. This usage goes back to ancient Latin rhetoric, in which *color* was a technical term for the shading of a set of facts by a skilled lawyer or other orator. (This usage is entirely distinct from that of color as ornamentation.[13])

Herbert was a specialist in the development of "colorable" or plausible arguments to support a given case. That was what a Renaissance ambassador did all the time, like his counterparts on the other side; thus, in one of his diplomatic dispatches Herbert notes that the canny Spanish diplomat Count Gondomar will apply "color . . . and deceit" in his account of current events.[14] His poems show Herbert doing the same thing: applying the orator's skills of exalting or blackening a given topic. (Note how the very language of rhetoric shades into the language of color.) And the colorable was the element in which the orator-poet Edward Herbert lived and wrote.

The Poems on Platonic Love

In a sequence of five poems, Herbert tried his hand at the most fashionable poetic topic of the period (the middle poem bears the date 1639): Platonic love. Rossi reads the sequence biographically as the story of a "very Platonic flirtation."[15] In several of the poems, Rossi finds a simplicity of style and humility of stance that he deems admirable (and infrequent) in Herbert. The poems, though, are rather wittier and tougher of mind than Rossi recognizes. Indeed, as might have been expected, they show many of the same strategies for using philosophy in love talk that have been observed above in the poems on black beauty.

Queen Henrietta Maria had brought with her from France the

précieuse tradition of a Platonic cult of female beauty. "It quickly took root in artificial court soil and flourished apace in the period preceding the wars. So popular were its manners that the whole court knelt in complimental worship of beauty in woman."[16] In a letter of 1634, James Howell writes: "The Court affords little News at present, but that there is a Love called Platonic Love, which much sways there of late; it is a Love abstracted from all corporeal gross Impressions and sensual Appetite, but consists in Contemplations and Ideas of the Mind, not in any carnal Fruition. This Love sets the Wits of the Town on work."[17] A modern historian of the movement reports that its literary "manifestations show courtly love jargon, with its emphasis upon *constancy, humbleness, service, beauty,* and *virtue;* some of them display the old idea of secrecy, much overripe rhetoric . . . [in summary] a congeries of stilted machinery."[18] This is the fashionable mode of writing that Herbert imitates with sly reservations.

Herbert's verse sequence. Herbert's first poem, "Platonic Love," glorifies the lady as an angel-like being, urging her not to deny her presence to the poet-speaker. In the second poem (identically titled), the speaker contrasts himself with callow youths who "love not Woman, but the Sex / And care no more than how themselves to please" (ll. 9–10). Mature fellows like the speaker are to be trusted.

> For while they from the outward sense transplant
> The love grew there in earthly mould, and scant,
> To the Soul's spacious and immortal field,
> They spring a love eternal, which will yield
> All that a pure affection can grant.
>
>   (st. 4)

The poem ends with a glimpse of the Platonic lovers in the afterlife, where they combine "those public joys, which are assigned / To blessed souls" (ll. 47–48) with the "contents they in each other find" (l. 50).

In paraphrase, "Platonic Love (II)" seems a typical product of courtly preciosity. And so a reader might deem it if reading the poem outside its sequence and without a sense of Herbert's tone and manner. Such a reader might even agree with Rossi in calling the work "the philosophical song of impotence."[19] A more careful reader will have picked up the mood from the opening stanza.

> Madam, believe't, Love is not such a toy,
> As it is sport but for the Idle Boy,
> Or wanton Youth, since it can entertain
> Our serious thoughts, and make us know how vain
> All time is spent we do not thus employ.

The sprightly rhythm and gamesome light texture intentionally undermine the solemnly self-dedicatory assertions. What we have here is the very opposite of abashed worship of the lady.

The third poem bears the title "The *IDEA*, Made of Alnwick in his Expedition to Scotland with the Army, 1639." It is the longest of the sequence and the most elaborate in argument. The title might seem an awkward conflation of the abstract Platonic Idea with the quotidian specifications of place and time. But that combination lies at the heart of this most amusing poem, which amounts to a survey of the different modes in which the Idea can be embodied in the everyday world.

Herbert begins with orthodox Platonism. "All Beauties vulgar eyes on earth do see, / At best but some imperfect Copies be, / Of those the Heavens did at first decree" (st. 1).

Of course, the conventional exposition goes on to remark, the material in which the Idea is embodied may in some measure deform its appearance (ll. 10–15). Nonetheless, it is generally the case that "fair is the mark of Good, and foul of Ill" (l. 25). As for the human body in particular, it is like a statue-maker's mold that is discarded when the statue "perfectly is cast" (l. 62).

> So when that form the Heavens at first decreed
> Is finished within, Souls do not need
> Their Bodies more, but would from them be freed.
>
> For who would still covered with their earth lie?
> Who would not shake their fetters off, and fly,
> And be, at least, next to, a Deity?
>
> However then you be most lovely here,
> Yet when you from all Elements are clear,
> You far more pure and glorious shall appear.
>
> Thus from above I doubt not to behold
> Your second self renewed in your own mold,
> And rising thence fairer than can be told.

> From whence ascending to the Elect and Blest
> In your true joys you will not find it least,
> That I in Heaven shall know and love you best.
>   (ll. 64–78)

The poem has at this point risen to the same otherworldly vision
that concluded "Platonic Love (II)." "The *IDEA*," though, does not
end at this point. Rather, with deliciously sardonic wit, Herbert
reminds the reader that the poet-speaker is a soldier on an expedition
that separates him from his beloved. His musings are fixed lovingly
on her physical form. (Herbert wants his reader to remember that
the Greek word *idea* literally means look, appearance.) "For while
I do your coming there [Heaven] attend, / I shall much time on
your Idea spend, / And note how far all others you transcend" (ll.
79–81).

The poem concludes by urging the lady not to rush into the next
world.

> Hasten not thither yet, for as you are
> A Beauty upon Earth without compare,
> You will show best still where you are most rare.
>
> Live all our lives then: If the picture can
> Here entertain a loving absent man,
> Much more th' Idea where you first began.
>   (ll. 88–93)

The poem that began with a lecture on Platonic copy-theory ends
with an erotic meditation on an entertaining picture. A witty de-
flation of pretense, the poem also stands as good Platonism—far
above the usual courtly productions. It reminds the reader of the
significance and worth Plato attributes to that fundamental craving
for beauty that he calls the divine Eros. For Platonism is an erotics
of knowledge that often takes rise from a knowledge of the erotic.

The next poem, "Platonic Love (III)," shows, according to Rossi,
a "tired" Herbert, "a humble and submissive lover."[20]

> Let her then be serene,
> Alike exempt from pity and from hate:
> Let her still keep her dignity and state;
> Yet from her glories something I shall glean,

> For when she doth them everywhere dilate,
> A beam or two to me must intervene.
>
> (ll. 31–36)

Rossi finds the verse "simple and inspired." Not surprisingly, he disparages the following poem, which notably qualifies the submissiveness found in "Platonic Love (III)." This concluding work of the sequence has no title, but Moore Smith labels it "An appeal to his senses not to fail him."[21]

The speaker calls upon his hopes not to despair. He admits his "presumption" (l. 7) in seeking to "love a Beauty which I should adore" (l. 10). But he retains hope that the lady will be more forthcoming.

> Would she then in full glory on me shine,
> An Image of that Light which is divine,
> I then should see more clear, while she did draw
> Me upwards, and the vapors 'twixt us awe:
> To open her eyes were to open mine,
> And teach me wonders which I never saw.
>
> (st. 6)

The lady would not be disparaging herself in granting her presence to him, since (the speaker argues with evident casuistry) "inequalities still most appear / When brought together and composed so" (ll. 41–42).

The poem concludes on this balanced note:

> Then hope, sustain thyself, though thou art hid
> Thou livest still, and must till she forbid;
> For when she would my vows and love reject,
> They would a Being in themselves project,
> Since infinites as they, yet never did,
> Nor could conclude without some good effect.
>
> (st. 9)

One could call this a lover's idolatry: he projects in his mind the image of the unattainable beauty. But the Platonism works differently here. It is the lover to whom are attributed the infinites of "vows and love"; it is their perfection that (in the overall harmony of things) produces a worthy object of love. Indeed, the ambiguous phrase "in themselves" suggests that they may themselves hold that "Being" they long for, just as the poem may be their "good effect." As is often the case with Herbert's love poems, this concluding passage of the sequence on Platonic love calls to mind major themes in the sonnets of Shakespeare. Herbert knowingly undercuts modish court Platonism: he reveals the fictions that underlie the lover's commitment, a commitment he nonetheless honors. The sequence can profitably be read as a dialogue of these two voices: the fashionable courtly and the truthful Shakespearean.

First and Last Poems

The present discussion of Herbert's later poems can conclude with what may well be his last, which in the 1665 edition bears the title "October 14, 1664." Since Herbert died in 1648, scholars have emended the numeral, Moore Smith to 1644, Rossi to 1646.[22] To see how far Herbert went in developing his poetic voice over perhaps four decades, one can compare the last poem with the first poem in the 1665 edition, which is "To his Watch, When he could not sleep."

That poem begins:

> Uncessant Minutes, whilst you move you tell
> The time that tells our life, which though it run
> Never so fast or far, your new begun
> Short steps shall overtake.

These minutes are "Death's Auditors" (l. 6); "for though life well / May scape his own Account, it shall not yours" (ll. 4–5).

"To his Watch" gives evidence of a keen ear for the musical matching of sound to sense (as in "short steps shall overtake"); one can imagine young George Herbert admiring (and learning from) the evident craftsmanship. But the work lacks an individual poetic voice; many authors of the period could adorn commonplaces with the same musicality.

In "October 14" one finds a vigor of utterance that is unmistakably that of the mature Herbert. He addresses the "Enraging Griefs" that strive among themselves to possess his heart. With sardonic indulgence he urges them to go about their destructive business more efficiently.

> For your own sakes and mine then make an end,
> In vain do you about a Heart contend,
> Which though it seem in greatness to dilate,
> Is but a tumor, which in this its state
> The choicest remedies would but offend.
>
> Then storm't at once, I neither feel constraint
> Scorning your worst, nor suffer any taint
> Dying by multitudes, though if you strive,
> I fear my heart may thus be kept alive,
> Until it under its own burden faint.
>
> (st. 2–3)

That last verse has a dying fall to it. But Herbert remains alive, remarking with mock exasperation, "What, is't not done?" (l. 16).

Now Herbert draws a moral from his experience of protracted dying.

> Why then, my God, I find,
> Would have me use you to reform my mind:
> Since through his help I may from you extract
> An essence pure, so spriteful and compact,
> As it will be from grosser parts refined.
>
> Which being again converted by his Grace
> To godly sorrow, I may both efface
> Those sins first caused you, and together have
> Your power to kill turned to a power to save,
> And bring my Soul to its desired place.
>
> (st. 4–5)

The argument recalls many poems of George Herbert in which earthly suffering is said to lift one toward God. Edward Herbert even uses terms that would have been appropriate in his brother's mouth: "Grace," "godly sorrow." The argument, though, is equivocal: a casual Christian reader will not notice that everything Herbert says fits perfectly into the author's non-Christian natural religion. Penance was a central article of Herbert's brief creed. So was a belief in a Providence that aids men in time of need. Careful readers of "October 14" would notice the complete absence of a mediator. Lord Herbert suffers his own purification, in no way imitating a prior Passion. And "those sins" seem to be his own doing—not offshoots of Adam's original sin that the mediator had to undo.

Upon analysis, this last poem, for all its realistic portrayal of an old man's burdened and breaking heart, is also a pointedly revised version of Christian poems about suffering and death (and the spiritual potentials of both) that Herbert knew very well. "October 14" is very different from the anguished theatrical passion with which Donne both welcomes and resists the saving force that overwhelms him. Nor is it much like the quaint surprise of George Herbert at noting the quickening action of grace that pangs him like growing pains.

What Herbert's poem shows is natural religion in action, purifying its leading proponent with no need of anything distinctively Christian. (Resemblances the casual reader may find to Christian beliefs simply point up Herbert's conviction that every religion bears the stamp of his five points.) Notice that it is Lord Herbert who— making use of the sorrows providentially provided by a cooperative deity—"reform[s]" his own "mind." It is he who "extract[s] an essence pure," he who "efface[s]" his "sins." This is not a Christian death and rebirth of the self; the speaker is, rather, pulling himself up by his moral bootstraps. In short, "October 14" is a deist version of Holy Dying. Cannily rewriting a kind of poem in which both his younger brother and the poetic mentor of his youth had excelled, Edward Herbert has mocked the developed system of belief (Christianity) that he deemed a mockery in turn of that simple "natural" creed by which men could live and die with consolation.

Chapter Seven

"An Ode upon a Question Moved"

None of Lord Herbert's poems has been so highly acclaimed as "An Ode upon a Question moved, Whether Love should continue for ever?" The author's "real masterpiece," A. Alvarez calls it.[1] Robert Ellrodt, in the most distinguished general study of the English metaphysical poets, writes that "the 'Ode' bears comparison with the most beautiful poems in English literature."[2] But critical discussion has not gone much further than commendation. Indeed, few English poems of such quality have been so ill-served by literary analysis.

One point has long been known. The "Ode" follows a pattern that Herbert found in one of Donne's greatest lyrics, "The Ecstasy." That pattern has been carefully laid out by George Williamson in his essay "The Convention of *The Extasie*": "description of the burgeoning of nature; description of lovers and their emotions; their absorption in the rapture of love; their relationship to some problem arising from this state of rapture; its investigation and solution; relation of the solution to their initial rapture."[3]

But Williamson, whose couple of pages on Herbert's "Ode" provide the best treatment in print, follows an odd procedure in his essay. He presents the poems related to Donne's poem not in chronological order, but in order of complexity. So one finds Herbert's "Ode" discussed before its indubitable source, Donne's "Ecstasy." This arrangement enables Williamson to avoid asking a vital question that no critic of Herbert has ever asked: what did the poet have in mind when he undertook this variation on a masterly poem by his longtime family friend?

And make no mistake—Donne was very much on Herbert's mind when he wrote the "Ode." No commentator seems to have remarked on the fact that in the *Occasional Verses*, which follow a general chronological order, the "Ode" begins on the leaf following that on which Herbert's memorial "Elegy for Doctor *Dunn*" concludes. It

will be the argument of the present chapter that the "Ode" constitutes Herbert's greatest tribute to the dead master. Herbert pays
that tribute by rewriting Donne's poem to accord with his own view
of this world and of the next. Unperplexing what Donne has willfully
and brilliantly tangled together, Herbert shows a love that is un-
mysterious but abiding, between lover and lass, as between poet
and his deceased predecessor.

Looking at the "Ode" by way of its author's deducible intention
allows one to avoid the absurd assertions that have been made by
casual commentators. J. B. Fletcher, for example, would have it
that Herbert's "Ode" "emasculates Donne to conformity with courtly
feminist propriety. . . . Donne's *Ecstasy* represents the virile mood
of platonic love, and Herbert's the effeminate, or feminist."[4] Comments that amount to the same thing are still being made. In a
recent history of English literature in the seventeenth century, one
can read that the "Ode" "is less physical than Donne's 'The Ecstasy.' "[5] That remark, like Fletcher's, is probably false, and certainly unhelpful to any reader seeking to appreciate Herbert's splendid
poem.

The Critique of Ecstasy

The word *ecstasy* comes from the Greek *ek-stasis*: "standing apart
from." In connection with mystical experience, the term designates
"a cataleptic state during which, the operations of the senses suspended, and the body in a state of suspended animation, the soul
is in direct intercourse with God."[6] Donne's poem uses this religious
sense of the word to portray another and more worldly variety of
ecstasy: that of human love.

In "The Ecstasy," the lovers' souls are said to have "gone out"
of their bodies to form an "abler soul." Donne imagines an observer
so purified as to be able to hear the single voice of this conjoint
soul. Standing "within convenient distance," this ideal observer
overhears the souls' voice urge them to return to their bodies, pre-
sumably to make love. This return to the flesh is explicitly presented
as a revelation.

> To our bodies turn we then, that so
> Weak men on love revealed may look;
> Love's mysteries in souls do grow,
> But yet the body is his book.

The poem concludes with the assertion, at once flip and fervent, that the ideal observer will "see / Small change, when we're to bodies gone."[7] Only souls (it was believed) are changeless, not bodies; but what distinguished this pair of souls was their perfect coupling, and that will also be the most notable mark of their reanimated bodies.

Now what would Herbert have made of Donne's poem? The first point to note is a lexical one. As might be expected from a philosopher of his views, Herbert was always hostile to any claim for knowledge derived from ecstasy. In *De Causis Errorum,* he argues that "revealed and ecstatic perception" should not be trusted because it leads to "innumerable hallucinations and impostures."[8] In his *Dialogue,* Herbert devotes a lengthy paragraph to "ecstasies," many of which (he believes) were "false, and made use of . . . to beguile the people." The word *ecstasy* in one form or another runs like a mocking refrain through this long passage, in connection with Arab and Greek, as well as with Christian, claimants to special insight derived through "trances" or "raptures."[9]

Another prose text can help clarify Herbert's approach to Donne's poem. This is Pierre Charron's *Of Wisdom* (1601). Herbert had a copy of the French original in his library.[10] A celebrated book in its day, "the breviary of unbelievers" (as a distinguished historian has called it[11]), *Of Wisdom* tends toward the abandonment of much of traditional religion in favor of the classical virtues. Charron "presents religion as an inferior and self-seeking morality, while a lay morality alone is worthy of a reasonable man." Charron "showed that there is a religion without morality, that of the devout; a morality without religion, that of the wise man; and a God without religion, that of deism."[12] Without question, Charron must have struck Herbert as a kindred spirit. In his chapter on the human soul, Charron distinguishes two kinds of separation of soul from the body. The first is the "natural" separation effected by death. The second is "not natural nor ordinary . . . . It is that which is done by ecstasies and ravishments." Charron is skeptical of these unnatural separations, attributing many to illness or to demons; he even doubts whether the examples in Scripture represent a true withdrawal of the soul or a mere suspension of its functioning.[13] And Charron's distinction between natural and unnatural separations was, one can readily believe, brought into Herbert's mind by Donne's poem.

What Herbert evidently did was to rewrite "The Ecstasy" with

this distinction in mind. Where Donne associated a joyful love with
the artificial ecstasy of a revealed religion, Herbert will associate it
with the natural separation of body from soul as expounded by a
natural religion. For Herbert, artificial ecstasy meant going out of
one's mind, especially through disease, superstition, or imposture.
Going out of the body is what one does at death and only then.
And one can depart with confidence that one's selfhood and love
will survive that separation—to prove which point Herbert had *De
Veritate* to fall back on.

Where Donne's "Ecstasy" is hyperbolic in argument, crackling
with wit and paradox, Herbert's "Ode" offers a serene surface, re-
vising out all assertions that will not pass the test set by *De Veritate*.
But this seeming blandness of tone is a mock naïveté, in which
Fletcher wrongly finds Herbert smoothing Donne away to conform
with courtly propriety. The implicit point is, rather, that Herbert's
few and simple religious beliefs are so manifestly correct that they
do not require the rhetorical fireworks of Donne's notoriously difficult poem.

Melander and Celinda

The "Infant-birth." Herbert's "Ode" opens with four qua-
trains of scene painting. The "well accorded Birds" sing "hymns"
to "welcome in the cheerful Spring" (st. 2).

> To which, soft whistles of the Wind,
> And warbling murmurs of a Brook,
> And varied notes of leaves that shook,
> An harmony of parts did bind.
>
> While doubling joy unto each other,
> All in so rare concent was shown,
> No happiness that came alone,
> Nor pleasure that was not another.
>   (st. 3–4)

The doubled pleasures prepare the way for the lovers, "*Melander*
and *Celinda* fair," who enter in the fifth stanza, "that mutually
happy pair" of whom it is true that "no happiness . . . came alone, /
Nor pleasure that was not another."

The one difficult moment in the introductory section of the "Ode" is the opening stanza, which presents a little riddle:

> Having interred her Infant-birth,
> The watry ground that late did mourn,
> Was strew'd with flow'rs for the return
> Of the wish'd Bridegroom of the earth.

Of course the bridegroom is the sun. But what is the "Infant-birth"? Grierson annotates as follows: "probably the snowdrops and earliest flowers. They had faded, and—as though Nature wept for them—a season of rain had followed."[14] Later critics have offered a better reading. The "Infant-birth" refers to the seed, buried in autumn and reborn in spring.[15]

Herbert's riddle evokes by way of contrast the opening lines of Donne's "Ecstasy"; "Where, like a pillow on a bed / A pregnant bank swelled up." These verses, so charged with sexuality, foreshadow the conclusion of Donne's poem. And Herbert's entire poem is also present, in germ, in his opening stanza. For Herbert was given to speaking of death as another birth. The analogy with his birth from the womb (one might say, his Infant-birth) consoled him with the expectation "to be transmitted to a more happy estate" by his death or later-birth, as he explains in his autobiography.[16] Herbert writes in *De Veritate:* "We have at present no more knowledge about the future than the knowledge we had of it in the womb. And this is in fact a fit comparison, for this world of external objects appears just as confined, meager and lowly to an exalted soul equipped with every kind of knowledge, as the womb does to a newly-born babe."[17] So the Infant-birth implies Herbert's view of death as a rebirth in a cycle of progressive advancement.[18]

There is still more to this image. Herbert would expect his readers to recall a passage in the New Testament. Paul writes that unless a seed dies, it cannot be reborn (1 Cor. 15:36ff.). The image serves Paul, as it does Herbert, to offer the consolation of survival after death. But typically, Herbert strips the image of anything distinctively Christian. He implies that it is the natural religion underlying Christianity that reassures man of an afterlife. Herbert's riddling images here are not parables that move men to confidence by way of Christ. The bridegroom of which Herbert speaks is the sun in heaven (figured as a bridegroom in Ps. 19:5); it is not the Son (traditionally in Christian symbolism the bridegroom of Church or Soul). Sun and seed are the natural things of the world, and they suggest to man's natural powers of reasoning that process of purification that is, Herbert believes, natural to man.

The consolation of philosophy.   Celinda breaks the silence of the lovers' peaceful embrace to give vent to her worry that death will put an end to their love. Joyed "To hear *Celinda* thus intent / To a love he so much did prize," Melander asks, in the central stanza of the poem,

> And shall our Love, so far beyond
> That low and dying appetite,
> And which so chaste desires unite,
> Not hold in an eternal bond?
>   (st. 18)

He offers a series of philosophical arguments to establish that, as the Song of Songs (8:6) has it, love is as strong as death. The Creation manifests the Creator, he notes; and men ascend to the invisible realm by way of the visible, adoring the Creator in his Creatures. Nor is it the case, Melander adds, that the "love and knowledge" we have on earth "take their end" with our life on earth (st. 22).

> O no, Belov'd, I am most sure,
> Those vertuous habits we acquire,
> As being with the Soul entire,
> Must with it evermore endure.
>
> For if where sins and vice reside,
> We find so foul a guilt remain,
> As never dying in his stain,
> Still punish'd in the Soul doth bide,
>
> Much more that true and real joy,
> Which in a vertuous love is found,
> Must be more solid in its ground,
> Than Fate or Death can e'r destroy.
>   (st. 23–25)

Melander's assumptions are those of *De Veritate*. There Herbert asserts that men are "not wholly extinguished by death" but survive by virtue of their intellectual faculties. And Herbert counts "Love among the intellectual and spiritual faculties"; indeed, he considers it our "foremost faculty." As a student of Plato, Herbert has learned the lesson of *The Symposium*: it is love that impels men to seek the absolute good. And even a virtuous physical love derives from that same love that directs us toward the realm of the invisible. So love is part of the deathless natural instinct that—by dictate of Nature—directs us toward "eternal blessedness." Love plays a key role in "the great unceasing work of nature": separating the corruptible from the incorruptible. (Thus, for Herbert, nature plays the role of grace.) Love moves us, whether we realize it or not, toward knowledge and blessedness. [19]

Accordingly, Melander can assure his beloved that

> These eyes again then, eyes shall see,
> And hands again these hands enfold,
> And all chaste pleasures can be told
> Shall with us everlasting be.
>
> (st. 28)

So far, Melander's philosophical consolation has derived from the defense of the immortality of the soul—a favorite topic of Renaissance disputation. Now Melander goes one step further. He argues that, even if the human soul were not by nature immortal, the lovers would make their souls immortal by their perfectly pure love (st. 31). This counterfactual proposition is as far as Herbert will go toward the paradoxicality of Donne.

The two succeeding stanzas evoke another aspect of Donne's style: the exquisite verse music he can obtain by playing learned polysyllables against a norm of breathlessly enraptured monosyllables.

> So when one wing can make no way,
> Two joined can themselves dilate,
> So can two persons propagate,
> When singly either would decay.

> So when from hence we shall be gone,
> And be no more, nor you, nor I,

> As one another's mystery,
> Each shall be both, yet both but one.
>   (st. 32–33)

The repetition of the stanza opening, "So when," suggests that the
poem has reached the climax of its argument, as do the multiple
echoes in these lines of Donne's poem (cf. in "The Ecstasy" vv. 12,
36, 71). The climax of Herbert's natural "mystery" comes, appropriately, in stanza 33, a number symbolic of resurrection. The
assertion made in this stanza would seem to require no paraphrase.
But it must be noted how the syntax allows for two possible readings
of the third line ("As one another's mystery"). At first one might
want to read: when we shall be gone and cease to be (as we have
been on earth) one another's mystery. That reading would correspond
to the situation of Donne's poem, in which the paradoxical unity
is presented as already accomplished. But Herbert's stanza ends in
such a way that, if one has thus misinterpreted the construction of
that third line, one must reread. The mysterious unity of the lovers
lies in the future, in the afterlife. Herbert's syntax here works out
in miniature what the entire poem is designed to effect: a correction
of Donne's mystifications, his confusions of earthly and supernatural
states of being.

    Some Influence.   The poem concludes quietly:

> This said, in her up-lifted face,
> Her eyes which did that beauty crown,
> Were like two stars, that having faln down,
> Look up again to find their place:
>
> While such a moveless silent peace
> Did seize on their becalmed sense,
> One would have thought some Influence
> Their ravished spirits did possess.
>   (st. 34–35)

The vagueness of "some Influence" is both moving and meaningful. *Influence* means literally "a flowing in"; the cosmos as a whole
in Herbert's poem (as in his philosophy) appears to be a massive
channel of benefits for man. The lovers are too involved with one
another to identify the particular source of their good fortune. But
for the reader of the poem, "some Influence" has a more specific

sense. Whose influence is it that has made this pair "one another's mystery" if not John Donne's? His recently ascended soul sheds (planetlike) its benevolent influence upon the lovers, and upon Edward Herbert's finest poem. The stellification of the honored dead is a familiar move in memorial poetry; rarely has it been used so delicately as it is here. Donne's errors of doctrine (as Herbert must have thought them) have been corrected: for us, in the poem; for Donne, by death into the reality of a natural religion that is inscribed in the benevolent structure of the world.

Chapter Eight

The Autobiography

The Critical Tradition

Among judgments of Herbert's autobiography, Swinburne's claim that it is one of the hundred best books ever written must stand at one end of the spectrum of opinion.[1] At the other end can be found Patrick Cruttwell's view that the "book, in spite of many passages which are undeniably, if unintentionally, amusing, seems at last a tedious and unpleasing work."[2] This might seem a large spread of opinion; in fact, however, a dreadful uniformity of judgment characterizes the critical tradition of the autobiography. Though some like it and some dislike it, virtually all critics agree on the nature of the work.

Long Herbert's most widely read book, the autobiography has for over two centuries been (in the words of R. D. Bedford) "the stumbling block to an appreciation of Herbert's real qualities."[3] A good part of the blame must be laid upon Horace Walpole, who first published Herbert's *Life* at his Strawberry Hill Press in 1764. Such twentieth-century scholars as Rossi and Bedford recognize the limitations of Walpole's interest in the autobiography; Rossi could not be clearer in condemning the "sickening Philistinism of Walpole."[4] Yet the very partial and biased appraisal of the autobiography enshrined in the prefatory matter to Walpole's first edition has misled even Rossi and Bedford—along with scores of other critics and readers. Indeed, it is difficult to think of another literary text of the English Renaissance that has been so widely read, widely admired, and thoroughly misunderstood.

Walpole was a specialist in chronicling and collecting the eccentric—not least in the lives and writings of the English nobility. His letters tell the story of his finding Herbert's unpublished manuscript at the home of a noble lady. Soon he was reading it aloud to assuage the grief of another (recently widowed) noble lady. "Gray and I read it to amuse her. We could not get on for laughing and screaming. I begged to have it in print. Lord Powis, sensible of the extravagance, refused. I insisted—he persisted. I told my Lady Hertford it was no matter, I would print it, I was determined. I sat down and wrote a flattering dedication to Lord Powis, which I knew he would swallow: he did, and gave up his ancestor." After publication, Walpole wrote that "the thing most in fashion is my edition of Lord Herbert's Life; people are mad after it."[5] Walpole responded to a fan letter from a noble correspondent: "I rejoice Lord Herbert has diverted you. I own, it appears to me the most singular book that ever was written. I am overpaid if it has answered my purpose in amusing you."[6]

In the prefatory matter to his edition, Walpole was as flattering as he could be. He "anticipate[s] the Reader's surprise. . . . He will find, that the History of Don Quixote was the Life of Plato." The book offers "foibles, passions, perhaps some vanity, surely some wrongheadedness" that its author "scorned to conceal, for he sought Truth, wrote on Truth, was Truth." Herbert's "descendants," Walpole adds, "desire the world to make this candid observation with them, 'That there must have been a wonderful fund of internal virtue, of strong resolution and manly philosophy, which in an age of such mistaken and barbarous galantry, of such absurd usages and false glory, could enable Lord Herbert to seek fame better founded, and could make him reflect that there might be a more desirable kind of glory than that of a romantic duellist.' "[7] Walpole is making gestures to placate the author's descendants, but it is clear where his interest in the book lies. It is in the "excesses and errors" of the author. As Rossi notes, Walpole views Lord Herbert as a conceited fool whose extravagances furnish an endless source of amusement.[8]

Walpole's prefatory matter had just the effect one would expect. He writes, "The caution with which I hinted at its extravagance, has passed with several for approbation, and drawn on theirs. . . . I do not wonder that Sir Philip Sidney was the darling hero, when Lord Herbert, who followed him so close and trode in his steps, is at this time of day within an ace of rivalling him."[9] The misreading of Sidney involved here has long ago been corrected; that of Herbert has survived to haunt his reputation.

Walpole's biased view has set the tone of critical comment on the autobiography up to the present—for admirers and disparagers alike. Most of the essays devoted to Lord Herbert pick up the comparison with the supposedly feckless Spanish Don. Thus a recent editor of the autobiography contends that "the knight-errant had, for the hours of composition, imprisoned the first of the deists."[10] One could cite a dozen similar remarks.

Perhaps the strongest statement of the standard reading is that of C. H. Herford in the preface to his edition of 1928. Herford notes the "enormous complacency" of the author: "this Jacobean man of fashion, who may be called with equal plausibility the last of the Knights errant and the first of the deists." Herford even brings up to date the Quixote/Plato analogy. "This *Herbert-Jekyll* . . . does not merely take possession alternately with *Herbert-Hyde* of the same bodily frame; they are quite cognizant of one another and take each other's existence as the most natural thing in the world. And though it is predominantly the image of one of them which flashes with extraordinary vividness from the pages of the *Life*, yet it is evident from some scattered touches, and even some entire pages, that the other was looking over the writer's shoulder, and on occasion borrowed the pen." For Herford, as for most critics, the merits of the *Life* are "mainly undesigned and unconscious." He finds "unconscious humor" all through the book.[11]

Like Herford, Margaret Bottrall insists on "Herbert's unconsciousness of his own absurdity."[12] And this is by no means the only argument (though it is the most common one) by which critics deny to Herbert any artistic consciousness in the *Life*. The American novelist William Dean Howells even went so far as to talk of the protagonist of the autobiography as if he were the creation of a historical novelist. "Thackeray himself could not have done it better, if he had been minded to portray a gentleman of the first James's time. . . . A rare sincerity marks the whole memoir, and gives it the grace of an antique simplicity." Howells professes himself delighted with the "picturesque and romantic" elements of the *Life*.[13]

Rossi's approach is different, but finally no less condescending to Herbert as autobiographer. He claims that the *Life* was dictated, in a spasmodic fashion, by an ill and weary old man, probably in the years 1643–44. Herbert (Rossi argues) put aside the manuscript after he had reached the time of his recall from Paris, at which point glowing nostalgia became less easy to sustain. After the forced departure from Montgomery Castle, Herbert no longer had the heart to return to the interrupted account. Rossi sees in the autobiography a document rich in pathos, but one intended only for Herbert's descendants. A work of utter sincerity, its absence of modesty would make it seem frivolous when it was published. In fact (Rossi holds), it is a work of confession intended only for the ears of later Herberts. [14]

Rossi breaks with the Walpole line in not laughing at the *Life*. Instead, it fills him with pity. But that response brings the reader no closer to a sense of the artistry at work and at play in the *Life*— to all those features that make it a typically Herbertian performance.

Private and Public Voices

The present chapter offers a fresh look at the autobiography. The standard view generally holds that the *Life* is radically incomplete; intended solely for its author's descendants; and inadvertent in its humor. For none of these contentions, though, is the evidence strong. The evidence is internal, and a reader who has come to understand how Herbert's writing generally functions will find the autobiography not at all what the critical tradition would lead one to expect. The authorial voice of this delightful book is not that of "the superlative coxcomb whose singular revelations made Gray and Walpole 'laugh and scream' " (Leslie Stephen), nor that of "a naive and ineffectual braggart" (Cruttwell). [15]

Like most of Herbert's prose, the *Life* speaks in two voices to two different audiences. The work begins in the voice of a family memoirist eager to furnish later generations of Herberts with useful information. Their "natural inclinations and humours" are likely to correspond to his own, so his "observations" will better guide them than "those vulgar rules and examples, which cannot in all points so exactly agree unto them." "I profess to write with all truth and sincerity," Herbert adds, "as scorning ever to deceive or speak false to any" (1). This opening passage offers the autobiography as a private document. In other often lengthy passages in the first quarter of the *Life*, this same voice provides a family history; an account of the ideal education for a gentleman; and advice on medicine and botany. And Herbert notes the characteristic temperament: "passion and choler, being infirmities to which our race is subject" (11; cf. 19).

If the opening page of the *Life* introduces the private voice, the book's conclusion could not be more thoroughly public in concern. Herbert's autobiography ends with an answered prayer. Herbert receives divine approval for the publication of *De Veritate,* and that book codifies the truths of religion devoid of all particular or private modifications.

The central portion of the book—devoted mainly to Herbert's life abroad—modulates from the predominantly private voice to the predominantly public one. Narrating his efforts "to make [him]self a citizen of the world as far as it were possible" (23), Herbert recounts first his military and amatory adventures, then his career as a diplomat. In a seemingly artless passage, Herbert puts into the mouth of the earl of Worcester the underlying movement of the autobiography. Reproving Herbert (at royal behest) for carrying on a personal feud likely to lead to an encounter at arms, "the Earl . . . told me" (Herbert writes) "that being now made ambassador, and a public person, I ought not to entertain private quarrels" (101).

Herbert presents himself as doing what Henry VIII failed to do; he subjects his "inclinations and humours"—his "passion and choler"—to the service of England and of Protestantism. Further widening the sphere of his activity, Herbert channels his temper into a biting critique of what he deems religious oppression. His commitment to truth is no longer a mere concern with veracity in family reportage; it becomes a commitment to the international publication of religious truths common to all members of the human family.

Herbert's biography of Henry VIII had been a tragic story told with bitter irony. The autobiography tells a comic story with wry self-directed humor. The Herbert who writes is not the same man as the Herbert whose acts are described. After all, the book ends with the decision to publish *De Veritate*. All the events recounted in the *Life* take place, so to speak, *ante veritatem*: before the coming of truth. Another way to put the point might be to say that Herbert looks upon his life *ante veritatem* much as the Christian looks at the Old Testament—as an anticipatory token of a future fulfillment. And the reader of the autobiography must think in a similar way. Every event narrated needs to be viewed in relation to the book's overall trajectory.

Duels and the Contest for Precedence

Walpole advised one correspondent to skip the first third of the *Life*:[16] the laughable "errors and excesses" begin with Herbert's escape from the clutches of domesticity to the masculine and military life of the French aristocracy. At that point the book becomes an amusing series of quaintly chivalric episodes. Or so most readers have taken it.

Indeed, nobody could hold back a smile when reading how Herbert, just arrived at Merlou in 1608, rescued a ribbon so rudely plucked by a "gentleman" from "a daughter of the Duchess [of Montmorency], of about ten or eleven years of age."

The young lady, offended herewith, demands her ribbon, but he refusing to restore it, the young lady, addressing herself to me, said, "Monsieur, I pray get my ribbon from that gentleman." Hereupon, going towards him, I courteously, with my hat in my hand, desired him to do me the honor, that I may deliver the lady her ribbon . . . again; but he roughly answering me, "Do you think I will give it you, when I have refused it to her?" I replied, "Nay then, sir, I will make you restore it by force"; whereupon also, putting on my hat and reaching at his, he to save himself ran away, and, after a long course in the meadow, finding that I had almost overtook him, he turned short, and running to the young lady, was about to put the ribbon on her hand, when I, seizing upon his arm, said to the young lady, "It was I that gave it." "Pardon me," quoth she, "it is he that gives it me." I said then, "Madam, I will not contradict you; but if he dare say that I did not constrain him to give it, I will fight with him." (49)

Herbert's efforts to obtain satisfaction on the field of honor prove unsuccessful when the duke of Montmorency expels the unnamed gentleman from his house.

The error here lies not in the reader's laughing, but in missing the fact that the author is laughing along all the way. The prim young Herbert is learning what the contest for honor means in a courtly society. Fought over a trifle, overseen by fickle nobles, often inconclusive—that contest nonetheless determines one's status in a land in which "scarce any man [was] thought worth the looking on, that had not killed some other in duel" (52).

In the course of the *Life*, though, Herbert's quarreling grows far more subtle. Fencing comes to seem a crude and unreliable way of resolving disputes. Most of Herbert's private feuds never reach the field of honor. They are ended by royal intervention or by the cowardice of the opposing party. And the very energy that the fighting-cock aristocrats throw into picking quarrels to bring them to the field of honor comes to seem an inappropriate overflow of sexual forces. The point is clear from a comic passage in which Herbert challenges the Frenchman Balagny, "saying I heard he had a fair mistress, and that the scarf he wore was her gift, and that I would maintain I had a worthier mistress than he, and that I would do as much for her sake as he, or any else durst do for his. Balagny hereupon looking merrily upon me, said, 'If we shall try who is the abler man to serve his mistress, let both of us get two wenches, and he that doth his business best, let him be the braver man' " (65). The young Herbert walks away from the Frenchman with disdain, but the author has made his point, mocking the endless maze of personal quarreling.

But if loving and warring overlap, so also do war and wit. As Herbert writes, "A man's wit is best showed in his answer, and his valor in his defense" (36). The passage goes on to compare warding off blows in fencing with the rhetorician's answering "affronts" in debate, and the analogy helps define the movement of the *Life*. Herbert (as public figure) will become a contestant for political status on behalf of his nation. The episodes are deadly serious in a Europe divided by war; but the transactions are no less absurd than those recounted in the episode of the ribbon. How Herbert played his role in the contest for prestige—and how he understood that role—become clear in an episode involving the Spanish ambassador to Paris.

The Spaniard was the natural rival of the English ambassador. And Herbert was particularly wary, remembering that "the Spanish ambassador had taken place of the English, in the time of Henry IV, in this fashion: They both meeting in an antechamber to the secretary of state, the Spanish ambassador, leaning to the wall in that posture that he took the hand of the English ambassador, said publicly, I hold this place in the right of the King my master; which small punctilio being not resented by our ambassador at that time, gave the Spaniard occasion to brag, that he had taken the hand from our ambassador." Herbert awaited "the occasion to right my master," which came when he and his retinue found themselves on the same road as the Spaniard and his party. Herbert puts himself and his counterpart through an elaborate comedy of actions, all designed to avoid receiving an affront. This passage conveys the tone of the encounter.

The Spanish ambassador seeing me approach, and imagining what my intention was, sent a gentleman to me, to tell me he desired to salute me;

which I accepting, the gentleman returned to the ambassador, who, alight-
ing from his coach, attended me in the middle of the highway; which
being perceived by me I alighted also, when, some extravagant compli-
ments having passed betwixt us, the Spanish ambassador took his leave
of me, went to a dry ditch not far off, upon pretence of making water,
but indeed to hold the upper hand of me while I passed by in my coach;
which being observed by me, I left my coach, and getting upon a spare
horse I had there, rode into the said dry ditch, and telling him aloud,
that I knew well why he stood there, bid him afterwards get to his coach,
for I must ride that way. (109–10)

Herbert goes on to apologize for recounting this event at such
length. "The Spaniards," he alleges, "do so much stand upon their
pundonores," their points of honor. In proof he cites "the answer
a Spanish ambassador made to Philip II king of Spain, who, finding
fault with him for neglecting a business of great importance in Italy,
because he could not agree with the French ambassador about some
such pundonore as this, said to him, 'How have you left a business
of importance for a ceremony!' The ambassador boldly replied to
his master, 'How, for a ceremony? your Majesty's self is but a
ceremony' " (110–11). The anecdote has particular relevance to the
time in which it was written (ca. 1643), as the Civil War in England
threatened the ceremony that constitutes kingship. But the anecdote
has a general significance within the autobiography as well. It brings
to a climax all the absurd strivings for precedence in which the
younger Herbert has engaged. The reader ought not doubt that the
autobiographer understands both the triviality of the object (a ribbon, a gesture of the hand) and the deadly earnestness of the game
played by the courtier / diplomat. The rueful comedy is not lost on
the author; it is his very subject. Like most points worth making
in Herbert's prose, though, it must be conveyed by indirection to
the knowing reader.

"Some Things Scarce Credible"

Having deflated the notion of ceremony, Herbert proceeds on the
same page, "I shall relate now some things concerning myself, which
though they may seem scarce credible, yet, before God, are true"
(111). The wonders he reports of himself will enthrall Herberts of
future generations as they look back with fascination at their uncommon progenitor. For the public reader, though, an altogether
larger story is being told.

The first prodigy concerns Herbert's growth. His tailor demands extra cloth to make him a suit, insisting that he has grown during his stay in France. The claim proves to be correct. Herbert attributes the unheard of increase in stature to a recent fever (111–12). But another suggestion has been planted in the mind of the alert reader. The years of the ambassadorship (during which he was writing *De Veritate*) were for Herbert years of extraordinary growth.

The next wonder he reports will also convey different points to different readers. No doubt many a reader has arched an eyebrow in disbelief upon encountering this passage: "It is well known to those that wait in my chamber, that the shirts, waistcoats, and other garments I wear next my body, are sweet, beyond what either easily can be believed, or hath been observed in any else, which sweetness also was found to be in my breath above others, before I used to take tobacco" (113). That last anecdotal detail of the tobacco ruining his breath is typical of how Herbert piles up information to carry the lazy reader on, without allowing time for interpretation. One can bask in the author's seemingly infinite complacency at his physical perfection. Or one can mock a man who, as the proverbial expression has it, likes the smell of his own excretions. This is the sort of passage that has led critics to speak of Herbert's childishly excessive self-regard. But the sweet smell of Herbert's flesh will elicit a richer interpretation in the canny reader who recognizes the context of thought in which Herbert is writing.

Herbert's younger contemporary, the saintly religious philosopher Henry More, reported a similar phenomenon of his own body. As his pupil Richard Ward wrote in *The Life of the Learned and Pious Dr. Henry More*: "He hath told us . . . that his breast and body, especially when very young, would of themselves send forth flowery and aromatic odors from them; and such as he daily almost was sensible of, when he came to put off his clothes and go to bed. And even afterwards when he was older, about the end of winter or beginning of spring, he did frequently perceive certain sweet and herbaceous smells about him, when yet there were no such external objects near, from which they could proceed."[17] The point of course is that More lived (as one still says) in the odor of sanctity.

A sweet odor emanating from the body traditionally betokened the presence of the divine, though a similar effect could derive from natural causes, as Cardan noted in his *On Subtlety*.[18] Herbert would have known of the way in which a freethinker like Vanini (executed

1619, the time of which Herbert is writing) interpreted the phenomenon of sweet sweat. Citing Plutarch's report of the delicious
odor with which Alexander the Great impregnated his garments,
Vanini argued that such seeming "miracles" were properly to be
attributed to the influence of nature.[19] The suggestion was that such
prodigies were generally either faked or real, but not supernatural.
Instances like that of Alexander were commonly adduced in the
course of the early seventeenth-century debate on the sources of
seeming miracles.[20]

The seeming unnaturalness of Herbert's sweet sweat takes its place
in a long tradition of religious polemics. Implicitly, Herbert is
attributing to himself a kind of sanctity; but it is the sanctity of a
natural man. As Charles Lyttle has noted, "the amazing egotism of
many passages in the *Autobiography* is to be attributed to the heightened self-consciousness of a prophet and apostle, rather than to petty
conceit." The significant sweat hints at what Lyttle calls Herbert's
"profound conviction, originating in . . . early manhood, that God
had appointed him to be the repristinator of his universal truth and
way of salvation and invisible catholic church, in direct succession
to the great moral philosophers of ancient days."[21] What Lyttle
misses, however, is the element of mockery that runs through Herbert's account. Herbert restores a natural life by parodying the
(unnatural) claims to unnatural prodigies. In so doing, he manifests
the divine in the everyday—his sweat finally proving as emblem-
atically meaningful as any of the objects that George Herbert mor-
alizes in his pious verses.

"A Gentle Noise from the Heavens"

No passage in Herbert's writing has aroused more critical disagreement than the climax of the *Life*. In the "loud though yet gentle"
thunder from a cloudless sky ("the serenest . . . that ever I saw"
[133–34]) Herbert professes to find divine approval of his publishing
De Veritate. John Leland had no doubt of the author's sincerity in
making this assertion.[22] A later eighteenth-century writer, Timothy
Dwight, was of another mind altogether. In "The Triumph of Infidelity" (1788), the American poet has Satan (tracing the historical
development of unbelief) report: "My Methodist, brave Herbert,
cried, / And whined, and wrote, pretended, prayed and lied." Dwight
adds a mock footnote (attributed to "Scriblerus") making the ref-

erence to the conclusion of the autobiography unmistakable. "See Lord Cherburg's Cock-Lane-Ghost Tale of Thunder's answer to Prayer."[23]

More recent commentaries have diverged no less widely. W. K. Jordan remarks of the passage in question, "We cannot possibly credit Herbert with sincerity in this amazing statement."[24] In his edition of the autobiography, Sidney Lee writes, "This testimony to a special divine revelation stangely contrasts with the advanced views that Herbert elsewhere advocates respecting the subject of Revelation" (134n).

On the other side, C. J. Webb argues that "there is nothing inconsistent in holding that the external authority of the record of revelation can add nothing to the testimony of natural reason, and yet in recognizing that to an individual such a personal experience as Herbert has recorded of himself may add something to it." Webb is persuaded that Herbert accepts "the possibility of direct communion between the soul and God. . . . It was just because he believed so decidedly in it that . . . the acceptance at second hand of other people's experiences seemed unnecessary to him."[25] Gawlick, too, sees no need to doubt Herbert's sincerity. He explains that Herbert's philosophy "does not exclude a private revelation by means of which a man can be freed from his doubt and stirred to the realization of a good purpose."[26]

The range of recorded opinion bespeaks the richness of this passage. Herbert's two voices come together to report the climactic moment of his life. A descendant seeking evidence of Lord Herbert's distinction can have no stronger witness than the cloudless heavens that spoke to him in the voice of the thunder. The student of Herbert's philosophy of religion can have no stronger witness of Herbert's sense of calling; the revelation was to Herbert, not to others. But that is true in a double sense: unlike the revelations hitherto brought forward to inaugurate new modes of religious practice, this one was binding on its recipient alone. It impelled him to publish a book exposing those unrevealed and sufficient truths inscribed (by a primordial natural revelation) in the heart of every individual. In a real sense, what Herbert recounts is a revelation to end all revelations. Nothing less would give him the courage to publish a "book . . . so different from any thing which had been written heretofore" by which he would (as he writes) "hazard myself to a general censure" (133).

The fact that Herbert's passage seems to mock the claims of personal revelation that became increasingly common in the Civil War years adds a touch of piquancy. As Rossi notes, Herbert composed the *Life* at a time when self-professed inspired prophets were rising up "at every street-corner"; Jordan had already recorded his "suspicion" that the autobiographer "made dexterous use of a pretension which the sects, whom Herbert disliked so intensely, were wont to employ for the advancement of their 'truth.' "[27] The claim of having received a personal message from the heavens would be conventional in Puritan autobiography. The tendency is to think of that genre as falling later in time than Herbert's *Life*, but at least one example was already at hand as he composed.

A Narration of the Life of Mr. Henry Burton (1643) is replete with episodes in which "the Lord puts strength in him in answer to a prayer." On one occasion Burton, having sought divine comfort, sees a rainbow, a vision he deems "supernaturall and miraculous." He calls it "my rainbow, as having the sole propriety in it, seeing it was seene of none but my selfe alone." This is one of "so many miracles, or miraculous deliverances" from which Burton has benefited; in them he professes to find a personal analogue to the deliverance of the English Church being carried forward (with divine aid) by the Puritans.[28]

Burton's text suggests the sort of claims that Herbert was guying. The revelation to Herbert fulfills and supplants other partial or feigned revelations. Like the surprisingly sweet sweat, the revelation shows the ironic force of Providence, teaching the true by parodying the false. The reader is trained (to cite the Chorus of Shakespeare's *Henry V*) in "minding true things by what their mockeries be."

Indeed, every feature of Herbert's seemingly simple report has a double significance. The serene cloudless sky, for example, serves to authenticate the miracle Herbert has received. Soon, however, the reader understands another meaning: Herbert's religion derives its authority not from fearful apprehension of the overcast heavens, but from the clear blue sky of reason.

Conclusion

Twentieth-century readers tend to expect an autobiography to furnish an introspective review of the author's life and times. Such readers have typically judged Herbert (in Paul Delany's words) "too invincibly complacent to produce an autobiography which advanced the art of introspection."[29] The problem here lies with the expectations brought to the *Life*. Beneath the genial voice of the family memoirist speaks the didactic voice of the prophetic reformer. The object of Herbert's autobiography is not to review the author's life, but to reform the reader into a proponent of natural religion. It was natural religion that gave form to Herbert's life, as it does to his autobiography.

Jonathan Goldberg has argued that even the most seemingly secular of early modern autobiographies show the pervasive influence (both structural and thematic) of spiritual autobiography and the kindred genre of the saint's life.[30] This is as true of Herbert's autobiography as of Cellini's or Cardan's. What is distinctive about Herbert's life is the way he organizes seemingly random, often picaresque episodes into a narrative that—by guying the saints of the old "particular" religion—manifests the hero of the new natural religion.

Chapter Nine
Herbert Then and Now

Most of the early comments on Herbert's books are hostile ones from pious authors who took up their pens to defend Christianity from the deist assault. To a late seventeenth-century professor of theology like the German Johannes Musaeus, Herbert's error was clear: he wrongly judged man's natural power sufficient to gain salvation. But, Musaeus insisted, Christ's sacrifice offers the sole remedy for man's innate sinfulness. A person who sought to be truly just on the basis of Herbert's five common notions of religion would be a "hypocrite."[1] Musaeus's Latin treatise is one of many directed against Herbert's philosophy of religion, which offered an inviting target for academic theologians.

Some vernacular critics resorted to amusingly ad hominem arguments. Richard Baxter, for one, adduced the example of George Herbert to cast doubt on Lord Herbert's account of cunning priestcraft. "You had a brother of your own, so holy a man, as his sincerity was past exception; and so zealous in his sacred ministry, as showed he did not dissemble."[2]

Another English author, Philip Skelton, mocked Herbert—not with his saintly sibling, but with his high place and title. In *Ophiomaches: Or, Deism Revealed* (1749), Skelton attacks "the self-sufficiency or deism of Lord Herbert." Using the dialogue form, Skelton puts the following into the mouth of a Christian apologist: "As the Christian religion was introduced into the world by men in the lowest rank of life, its great adversary, deism, owes its origin, at least among us, to a man of quality. . . . The honor and admiration, with which high birth and titles are revered, were derived upon deism through the dignity of its author." Nonetheless, Skelton goes on to note with much complacency, "Christianity, notwithstanding its humble genius and contemptible appearance, went farther up among mankind, and against the stream, than deism . . . with all its pomp and borrowed aids, went downward. For the sufficiency of God, is infinitely more powerful than the self-sufficiency of man."[3]

In comparison with Skelton's gibing, Leland's judgment of Herbert (also from the mid-eighteenth century) is a model of fairness. "He may be justly regarded as the most eminent of the deistical writers, and in several respects superior to those that succeeded him. He may be also considered as the first remarkable deist in order of time, that appeared among us as a writer in the last century. . . . His Lordship seems to have been one of the first that formed deism into a system, and asserted the sufficiency, universality, and absolute perfection of natural religion, with a view to discard all extraordinary revelation as useless and needless."[4]

As Leland's remarks indicate, deism became widespread in the eighteenth century. Indeed, the doctrines of deism are congruent with the central tenets of Enlightenment thought, as Arthur Lovejoy demonstrates in his classic paper "The Parallel of Deism and Classicism."[5]

For the period after Leland, a study of Herbert's reputation as a theorist of religion would be a general history of comments on deism. Positions that Herbert had adopted, rhetorical procedures that he had developed to insinuate his views—these became commonplace. So widespread was deism that one can rarely pick out this or that idea and with confidence say that it was taken from Herbert in particular. But there is no doubt that Herbert was being read. In Colonial America, Herbert's name appears in many library catalogs, along with such later English deist authors as Charles Blount and Anthony Collins.[6] But if the specific chains of direct influence are difficult to establish, the general likenesses are unmistakable. To cite only one example, the standard book on deism in Colonial America says of Benjamin Franklin that "in spite of his reticence in respect to deism, Franklin said enough, chiefly in confidential letters, to warrant his classification as a deist along the general lines of Lord Herbert of Cherbury."[7]

Even in the Revolutionary Age, as this last remark suggests, deism was a philosophy that could not with impunity give public utterance to its full set of doctrines. Much of the story of deism is a story of beliefs half-uttered, half-suggested. The risks of publication were considerable. The brilliant physicist Isaac Newton wrote a treatise of pagan theology in which he adopts a position closer to that of a deist like Herbert than to any form of Christianity. Newton intended this to be his masterpiece, according to Richard Westfall, but he never published it; indeed, the manuscript remains un-published.[8]

The example of Newton serves to remind Herbert's readers of the constraints under which he wrote. One cannot overestimate the importance for Herbert of the need to conceal and reveal at the same time. Herbert's thrusts at Christianity did not go unnoticed, but they were all implicit or indirect.

As the present volume has sought to show, the techniques of purposeful obliquity that Herbert learned in his diplomatic career served him well when he came to write on religion. Herbert's char-acteristic texts manifest to the careful reader a studied doubleness. The bland surface sense heightens the piquancy of the covert sense that the text is designed to insinuate into the reader's mind. This is true of *De Veritate*, of the biography of Henry VIII, and of the autobiography as well. Making a virtue of necessity, Herbert turned constraint into artful form, obligatory concealment into a provo-cation to independent thought. He earned his place in the company of the major deists—all of them (in Peter Gay's words) "powerful agents of modernity."[9]

Future readers of Herbert may wish to carry forward the venture begun by Margaret Fuller in her essay "The Two Herberts." This piece has, to be sure, its cloying period touches. On "an afternoon of one of the longest summer days," Edward and George Herbert are imagined meeting on a country lane. With the chatty philo-sophizing of early adolescence, the two gifted adults exchange opin-ions on the nature of human life. Each illustrates his point of view with readings from his own verses, to which the other listens thoughtfully.

Thus when Edward reads (in Fuller's translation) his Latin poems "Life" and "Conjectures Concerning the Heavenly Life," George responds: "The flood of your thought has swept over me like music and like that, for the time, at least, it fills and satisfies." He then goes on to criticize what is absent from Edward's vision: "the depths of love and sorrow made known to men, through One whom you as yet know not."[10]

For all the purple passages in her essay, Margaret Fuller must be given credit for recognizing "the sprightly, fresh, and varied style of Lord Herbert." For Fuller, Herbert is no coxcomb, no buffoon; he is a Hamlet-like figure. "In his eye, and in the brooding sense of all his countenance, was felt the life of one who, while he deemed that his present honor lay in playing well the part assigned him by destiny, never forgot that it was but a part, and fed steadily his forces on that within that passes show."[11]

At one point in the fictional dialogue she composes for the two brothers, Fuller has George Herbert offer an objection to his brother's thought that will be familiar to readers of the scholarship devoted to Edward Herbert. After asserting that "the progress of the mind should be from natural to revealed religion," George asks, "Of your own need of such, did you not give convincing proof, when you prayed for a revelation to direct whether you should publish a book against revelation?" Lord Herbert replies: "You borrow that objection from the crowd, George; but I wonder you have not looked into the matter more deeply. Is there anything inconsistent with disbelief in a partial plan of salvation for the nations, which, by its necessarily limited working, excludes the majority of men up to our day, with belief that each individual soul, wherever born, however nurtured, may receive immediate response, in an earnest hour, from the source of truth[?]"

George replies: "But you believed the customary order of nature to be deranged in your behalf. What miraculous record does more?" To this Edward answers: "It was at the expense of none other. A spirit asked, a spirit answered, and its voice was thunder; but, in this, there was nothing special, nothing partial wrought in my behalf, more than if I had arrived at the same conclusion by a process of reasoning."[12]

For all its sentimentality of scene and language, Fuller's essay makes a case that needed, and still needs, to be made for Edward Herbert as a thinker and artist fully deserving of mention alongside his now much-talked-about younger brother.

Notes and References

Preface

1. Ben Jonson, "To Sir Edward Herbert," *Epigrams*, in *The Oxford Jonson*, ed. C. H. Herford, P. & E. Simpson (Oxford, 1925–51), 8:68. Spelling regularized, as throughout the present volume, in quotations from early modern English. The poem was first published in 1616.

2. Christian Kortholt, *De Tribus Impostoribus Magnis Liber* (Kiel, 1680), 4–92.

3. Voltaire, "Lettre sur les auteurs anglais" in *Oeuvres complètes de Voltaire*, vol. 26 (Paris, 1879), 482. This and all other unattributed translations are by the present author.

4. John Leland, *A View of the Principal Deistical Writers* (London, 1754), 4–5.

5. Gotthard Victor Lechler, *Geschichte des englischen Deismus* (1841; reprint, Hildesheim, 1965), xliii–xliv.

6. John W. Bicknell, "Leslie Stephen's 'English Thought in the Eighteenth Century': A Tract for the Times," *Victorian Studies* 6 (1962): 118–19.

7. Leslie Stephen, "Lord Herbert of Cherbury," *National Review 35* (1900): 670, 673, 669.

8. Mario M. Rossi, *La vita, le opere, i tempi di Edoardo Herbert di Chirbury* [Rossi prefers this spelling], 3 vols. (Florence, 1947). Further references to this work will be to Rossi, *La vita*, volume 1, 2, or 3.

9. W. B. Yeats, introduction to J. M. Hone and M. M. Rossi, *Bishop Berkeley: His Life, Writings & Philosophy* (New York, 1931), xxix.

10. Mario M. Rossi, *A Plea for Man* (Edinburgh, 1956), 158–59, 163–64.

11. Mario M. Rossi, *Verso una teologia* (Bari, 1946), 171–73.

Chapter One

1. Rossi makes a good case for 1582 as against the traditional date of 1583; see "The Birth Date of Lord Herbert of Cherbury," *Modern Language Notes* 63 (1948), 144.

2. *Herbert Correspondence*, ed. W. J. Smith (Cardiff, 1963), 3.

3. Smith, ed., *Correspondence*, 3–4.

4. *The Autobiography of Edward, Lord Herbert of Cherbury*, ed. Sidney Lee (London, 1906; reprint, Westport, Conn. 1970), 3. Further references

to this work in the present chapter will appear parenthetically in the text as Lee.

5. J. E. Neale, "Three Elizabethan Elections," *English Historical Review* 46 (1931): 238.

6. H. W. Garrod, "Donne and Mrs. Herbert," *Review of English Studies* 21 (1945): 171.

7. Rossi, *La vita*, 1:39.

8. Ibid., 45.

9. Amy M. Charles, *A Life of George Herbert* (Ithaca, 1977), 36–43.

10. Charles, *A Life*, 57–59.

11. See John Walter Stoye, *English Travellers Abroad: 1604–1667* (London, 1952), esp. chap. 1.

12. Maurice Magendie, *La Politesse Mondaine . . . de 1600 à 1660*, vol. 1 (Paris, 1925), 54.

13. Joseph Hall, *Quo Vadis?* (London, 1617), fifth page of unpaged dedication; 83, 85.

14. René Pintard, *Le Libertinage érudit*, vol. 1 (Paris, 1943), 565.

15. Pintard, 1: 5.

16. Magendie, *La Politesse*, 1:112–13.

17. Ibid., 117.

18. Rossi, *La vita*, 1:115.

19. Edmund H. Dickerman, "Henry IV of France, the Duel and the Battle Within," *Societas* 3 (1973): 207–8.

20. Magendie, *La Politesse*, 1:67.

21. Stoye, *English Travellers*, 61.

22. Guillaume de Chevalier, *A most necessarie Discourse of Duels*, trans. T. Heigham (Cambridge, 1624), 4.

23. Dickerman, "Henry IV," 209, 215.

24. Frederick R. Bryson, *The Sixteenth-Century Italian Duel* (Chicago, 1938), 83.

25. William Segar, *The booke of honor and armes* (London, 1590), sig. A2–A2v.

26. James Cleland, *The Institution of a Young Noble Man* (Oxford, 1607; reprint, New York, 1948), 233.

27. Norbert Elias, *The Court Society*, trans. Edmund Jephcott (Oxford, 1983), 100, 94, 115.

28. Rossi, *La vita*, 1:141.

29. Elias, *Court Society*, 108.

30. Rossi, *La vita*, 1:212.

31. Ibid., 262–63.

32. J. R. Jones, *Britain and Europe in the Seventeenth Century* (New York, 1966), 4.

33. Rossi, *La vita*, 1:268.

34. Garrett Mattingly, *Renaissance Diplomacy* (1955; reprint, Baltimore, 1964), 204.

35. Rossi, *La vita*, 2:23. The book-length chapter Rossi devotes to the diplomatic years is without question the strongest and most valuable section of his monograph. Not coincidentally, it is the only chapter in which the Italian is on Herbert's side. Ever the moralist, Rossi sees Herbert as more upright and just than the men he dealt with, or the master he served (Rossi, *La vita*, 2:258). In *The Defence of Truth* (Manchester, 1979), 22–23, R. D. Bedford comments acutely on Rossi's identification with Herbert the diplomat.

36. Rossi, *La vita*, 2:170.

37. S. L. Adams, "Foreign Policy and the Parliaments of 1621 and 1624," in *Faction and Parliament*, ed. Kevin Sharpe (Oxford, 1978), 146.

38. Samuel R. Gardiner, ed., *Letters . . . Illustrating the Relations between England and Germany at the Commencement of the Thirty Years War*, 2d ser. (London, 1868), 13.

39. Rossi, *La vita*, 2:90, 92–93.

40. Gardiner, ed., *Letters*, 160.

41. Roy E. Schreiber, *The Political Career of Sir Robert Naunton 1589–1635* (London, 1981), 76. On the structure of Jacobean diplomacy, I follow Schreiber, passim.

42. Conrad Russell, *Parliaments and English Politics 1621–29* (Oxford, 1979), 420–21.

43. Rossi, *La vita*, 365.

44. *Collections Historical and Archaeological Relating to Montgomeryshire . . .* Vol. 20 (1886), 110.

45. Sir Henry Wotton, quoted in Mattingly, *Diplomacy*, 206.

46. Mattingly, *Diplomacy*, 186.

47. Gardiner ed., *Letters*, 113.

48. *Montgomeryshire Collections* 20:259.

49. Ibid.; Rossi, *La vita*, 2:173.

50. *Mongomeryshire Collections* 20:266.

51. Rossi, *La vita*, 2:397–98.

52. A. H. Dodd, *Studies in Stuart Wales*, 2d ed. (Cardiff, 1971), 78–79.

53. Rossi, *La vita*, 2:423.

54. Rossi, *La vita*, 2:464.

55. Joseph Berington, *The Memoirs of Gregorio Panzani* (Farnborough, 1970), fourth and sixth pages of unpaged introduction by T. A. Birrell to this reprint of the 1793 edition.

56. Rossi, *La vita*, 2:498–99.

57. William Stephens, *An Account of the Growth of Deism in England* (London, 1696), 10.

58. *Reactions to the English Civil War 1642–1649*, ed. John Morrill (London, 1982), 73, 229.

59. J. S. Morrill, *The Revolt of the Provinces: Conservatives and Radicals in the English Civil War 1630–1650* (London, 1976), 90.

60. *Montgomeryshire Collections,* Vol. 22 (1888), 170.

61. Ronald Hutton, *The Royalist War Effort 1642–1646* (London, 1982), 150.

62. *Montgomeryshire Collections* 22:185.

63. Evelyn G. Rogers, "The Death of Lord Herbert of Cherbury," *Notes and Queries* 226 (1981):524.

64. William Empson, "A Deist Tract by Dryden," *Essays in Criticism* 25 (1975):89.

65. John McManners, *Death and the Enlightenment* (Oxford, 1981), 264, 266.

66. *Aubrey's Brief Lives*, ed. Oliver Lawson Dick (1949; reprint, Ann Arbor, 1962), 135.

67. *The Table-Talk of John Selden*, ed. S. W. Singer (London, 1860), 237.

68. John Donne, *The Complete English Poems*, ed. A. J. Smith (Harmondsworth, 1973), 218–19.

Chapter Two

1. Rossi, *La vita*, 3:287.

2. *De Veritate*, trans. Meyrick H. Carré (Bristol, 1937), 15–16. Further references to this volume in the present chapter will be given parenthetically in the text.

3. Meyrick H. Carré, *Phases of Thought in England* (Oxford, 1949), 221–22.

4. Mario M. Rossi, "The Nature of Truth and Lord Herbert of Cherbury's Inquiry," *The Personalist* 21 (1940): 249–50.

5. Charles de Rémusat, *Lord Herbert de Cherbury* (Paris, 1874), 181.

6. Charles Lyttle, "Lord Herbert of Cherbury, Apostle of Ethical Theism," *Church History* 4 (1935): 254–55.

7. R. D. Bedford, *The Defence of Truth: Herbert of Cherbury and the Seventeenth Century* (Manchester: Manchester University Press, 1979), 77.

8. Richard H. Popkin, *The History of Scepticism from Erasmus to Descartes* (1964; rev. ed., New York, 1968), 1, 12. The next three paragraphs are based on Popkin.

9. *A Journal of . . . Monsieur de Maisse . . .*, trans. G. B. Harrison and R. A. Jones (London, 1931), 58.

10. Conrad Russell, "Arguments for Religious Unity in England, 1530–1650," *Journal of Ecclesiastical History* 18 (1967): 216.

11. W. K. Jordan, *The Development of Religious Toleration in England*, vol. 1 (1932; reprint, Gloucester, Mass., 1965), 335–36. Cf. Joseph Lecler, S.J., *Toleration and the Reformation*, vol. 1, trans. T. L. Westow (London, 1960), 369–76.

12. The present paragraph draws upon Mario Sina, *L'avvento della ragione: 'Reason' e 'above Reason' dal razionalismo teologico inglese al deismo* (Milan, 1976), 150–59.

13. Hugo Grotius, *True Religion* (London, 1632; facsim. reprint, Amsterdam, 1971), 129.

14. Sina, *L'avvento della ragione*, 153, 158.

15. A. R. Winnett, "Were the Deists 'Deists?' " *Church Quarterly Review* 161 (1960): 70–77.

16. *The Dictionary Historical and Critical of Mr. Peter Bayle*, vol. 5 (London, 1738), 482.

17. Quoted in Henri Busson, *La Pensée religieuse française de Charron à Pascal* (Paris, 1933), 89.

18. *The Works of President Edwards*, vol. 1 (New York, 1843), 467.

19. *Oeuvres complètes de Bossuet*, vol. 14, ed. F. Lachat (Paris, 1863), 203.

20. Richard Bentley, *Eight Boyle Lectures on Atheism* (1692; facsim. reprint, New York, 1976), 6.

21. Don Cameron Allen, *Doubt's Boundless Sea: Skepticism and Faith in the Renaissance* (Baltimore, 1964), vi.

22. George H. Sabine, "The *Colloquium Heptaplomeres* of Jean Bodin," in *Persecution and Liberty: Essays in Honor of George Lincoln Burr* (1931; reprint, New York, 1968), 271–72.

23. Roland N. Stromberg, *Religious Liberalism in Eighteenth-Century England* (Oxford, 1954), 55.

24. Stephens, *Deism in England*, 4.

25. G. E. Aylmer, "Unbelief in Seventeenth-Century England," in *Puritans and Revolutionaries*, ed. Donald Pennington and Keith Thomas (Oxford, 1978), 22.

26. See Louis Bredvold, "Deism before Lord Herbert," *Papers of the Michigan Academy of Science, Arts and Letters* 4 (1924): 431–42.

27. Leland, *A View*, 2; [iii].

28. Ibid., 7–8.

29. Richard Baxter, *More Reasons for the Christian Religion* (London, 1672), 80.

30. *The Philosophical Writings of Richard Burthogge*, ed. Margaret W. Landes (Chicago, 1921), 36. The passage is from *Organum Vetus et Novum* (London, 1678).

31. Rossi, *La vita*, 1:582; cf. 1:423.

32. This passage is one of the additions made by the author to the 1645 printing of *De Veritate*. These make explicit the implications of the original text. On the additions, see *De Veritate*, Gawlick facsim., 1:xxxiii–xxxiv, xliv.

33. Kortholt, *De Tribus Impostoribus*, 84.

34. Ibid., 59, 33, 92.

35. Wilhelm Dilthey, "Die Autonomie des Denkens . . . im 17. Jahrhundert," in his *Weltanschauung und Analyse des Menschen seit Renaissance und Reformation* (1914; reprint, Stuttgart, 1960), 254.

36. Bedford, *The Defence of Truth*, esp. chapter 4.

37. Ernst Cassirer, "Wahrheitsbegriff und Wahrheitsproblem bei Galilei," *Scientia* 62 (1937): 186–87. (The essay appears in French translation in the supplement to this volume of *Scientia;* the corresponding passage is on pp. 70–71 of the supplement.)

38. Peter Gay, *Deism: An Anthology,* (Princeton, 1968), 9.

39. Thomas Halyburton, *Natural Religion Insufficient* (1714; reprint, Philadelphia, 1798), xiii, 68, 66.

40. Ibid., 266, 267.

41. Ibid., 261.

42. Gay, *Deism,* 11–12.

Chapter Three

1. On the dates of composition, see Rossi, *La vita,* 3:504–7.

2. *De Veritate,* Gawlick facsim., 1:xliv.

3. Quotations in this paragraph are from Roger L. Emerson, "King-Craft, Priest-Craft and Other Conspiracies," *Enlightenment Essays* 3 (1972): 7–17.

4. *Lord Herbert of Cherbury's "De Religione Laici,"* trans. Harold R. Hutcheson (New Haven, 1944), 87. Further references to this work in the present chapter appear parenthetically in the text.

5. *The Antient Religion of the Gentiles,* trans. William Lewis (London, 1705); further references to this work in the present chapter will appear parenthetically in the text.

6. Richard S. Westfall, "Isaac Newton's *Theologiae Gentilis Origines Philosophicae,"* in *The Secular Mind: Transformations of Faith in Modern Europe,* ed. W. Warren Wagar (New York, 1982), 22.

7. Don Cameron Allen, *Mysteriously Meant* (Baltimore, 1970), 69.

8. Gerardus Vossius, *De Theologia Gentili,* vol. 1 (Amsterdam, 1641; facsim. reprint, New York, 1976), 118, 142.

9. Ibid., 22

10. Philip Skelton, *Ophiomaches: Or, Deism Revealed,* vol. 2 (London, 1749), 312.

11. Allen, *Mysteriously Meant*, 77.

12. Clement Webb, *Studies in the History of Natural Theology* (Oxford, 1915), 350.

13. Heinrich Scholz, *Die Religionsphilosophie des Herbert von Cherbury* (Giessen, 1914), 21.

14. D. P. Walker, *The Ancient Theology* (London, 1972), 164–93; the quotation is from 185.

15. John Orr, *English Deism: Its Roots and its Fruits* (Grand Rapids, 1934), 67–68, 66.

16. Kortholt, *De Tribus Impostoribus,* 83–85.

17. Allen, *Mysteriously Meant,* 78.

18. Hutcheson, introduction to *De Religione Laici,* 46.

19. Mario M. Rossi, *Alle fonti del deismo e del materialismo moderno* (Florence, 1942), 94n. See also Rossi, *La vita,* 3:153n, 530–33.

20. Opening paragraph of the unpaged advertisement that begins the 1768 edition of the *Dialogue,* Gawlick facsim., vol. 3.

21. Lyttle, "Lord Herbert," 261, 259.

22. Ibid., 262.

23. Günter Gawlick, "Abraham's Sacrifice of Isaac Viewed by the English Deists," *Studies on Voltaire and the Eighteenth Century* 56 (1967): 577–81.

24. Ibid., 577.

Chapter Four

1. W. Moelwyn Merchant, "Lord Herbert of Cherbury and Seventeenth-Century Historical Writing," *Transactions of the Honourable Society of Cymmrodorion* (1956), 53, 60.

2. *The Expedition to the Isle of Rhé by Edward Lord Herbert of Cherbury,* ed. Lord Powis (London, 1860), xxix. Further references to this work in the present chapter are given parenthetically in the text.

3. Roger Lockyer, *Buckingham* (London, 1981), 397.

4. Ibid., 402–3.

5. Merchant, "Historical Writing," 57.

6. Mario Rossi, "Lo sbarco inglese nell'Isola de Ré (1627) e la polemica militare nel XVII secolo," *Nuova Rivista Storica* 21 (1937): 138.

7. The dedicatory epistle to the king is cited from the first edition of *The Life and Reign* (London, 1649), sig. A2. Citations to the body of the history will be to the more accessible reprint published by Alexander Murray (London, 1870); in the present chapter these will appear parenthetically in the text.

8. *The Works of John Locke,* vol. 3 (London, 1812), 274–75; the work was first published in 1720.

9. J. R. Hale, *The Evolution of British Historiography* (Cleveland, 1964), 11.

10. Quoted in A. G. Dickens, "Johannes Sleidan and Reformation History," in *Reformation, Conformity and Dissent: Essays in Honour of Geoffrey Nuttall*, ed. R. Buick Knox (London, 1977), 26.

11. Quoted in Francis Bacon, *The History of the Reign of King Henry VII*, ed. F. J. Levy (Indianapolis, 1972), 43, 32.

12. F. J. Levy, *Tudor Historical Thought* (San Marino, Calif., 1967), 267.

13. S. L. Goldberg, "Sir John Hayward: 'Politic' Historian," *Review of English Studies* 6 (1955):242.

14. The fictional speeches were first remarked upon by H. A. L. Fisher, "The Speeches in Lord Herbert of Cherbury's *Life and Reign of Henry VIII*," *English Historical Review* 20 (1905):498.

15. In the margins of his copy of the 1649 edition, Jonathan Swift wrote alongside the latter passage, "The author means himself and [h]is own style." See Swift's *Works*, vol. 5, ed. Herbert Davis (Oxford, 1962), 247.

16. *Autobiography*, ed. Lee, xxxviii.

17. *Life and Reign*, ed. Murray, 105.

18. Merchant, "Historical Writing," 60–61.

19. Rossi, *La vita*, 2:513.

20. A. F. Pollard, *Henry VIII* (1905; reprint, New York, 1966), xxvi, 214–15.

21. Rossi, *La vita*, 2:510.

22. Quoted in J. J. Scarisbrick, *Henry VIII* (Berkeley, 1968), 526.

23. Sanders and Burnet are quoted from Arthur J. Slavin, ed., *Henry VIII and the English Reformation* (Lexington, Mass., 1968), 11, 20.

24. Slavin, *Henry VIII*, viii–ix.

25. Bacon, *History*, ed. Levy, 247.

26. Judith H. Anderson, *Biographical Truth: The Representation of Historical Persons in Tudor-Stuart Writing* (New Haven, 1984), 197.

Chapter Five

1. *The Poems English and Latin of Edward Lord Herbert of Cherbury*, ed. G. C. Moore Smith (Oxford, 1923), xvii. All quotations of Herbert's verse in the present volume are taken from this edition.

2. *The Poems of Lord Herbert of Cherbury*, ed. John Churton Collins (London, 1881), xviii.

3. Stephen, "Lord Herbert," 661.

4. Rossi, *La vita*, 1:201, 205, 192–93.

5. R. G. Howarth, ed., *Minor Poets of the Seventeenth Century* (London, 1931), xi.

6. A. Alvarez, *The School of Donne* (New York, 1961), 60.

7. Patrick Cruttwell, *The Shakespearean Moment* (London, 1954), 166–67, 173, 169.

8. Robert Ellrodt, *Les Poètes métaphysiques anglais,* vol. 2 (Paris, 1960), 54–60.

9. Donne, *Complete English Poems,* ed. Smith, 187.

10. Étienne de la Boétie, *Discours de la servitude volontaire,* ed. S. Goyard-Fabre, (Paris, 1983), 136.

11. J. W. Williamson, *The Myth of the Conqueror* (New York, 1978), 29 and passim.

12. *The Oxford Jonson,* ed. Herford and Simpson, 1:136.

13. Ruth Wallerstein, *Studies in Seventeenth-Century Poetic* (Madison, 1950), 82; Barbara Lewalski, *Donne's "Anniversaries" and the Poetry of Praise* (Princeton, 1973), 325.

14. Edward Forset, *A comparative discourse of the bodies natural and politique* (London, 1606), 99–100.

15. James V. Mirollo, *The Poet of the Marvelous: Giambattista Marino* (New York, 1963), 123.

16. Frank J. Warnke, "Marino and the English Metaphysicals," *Studies in the Renaissance* 2 (1955): 167–70. Mirollo, *Poet of the Marvelous,* 253–55, shows that Herbert also drew upon Marino's source in the Spanish poet Lope de Vega.

17. Ellrodt, *Les Poètes métaphysiques anglais,* vol. 2, 39–40.

18. Mary Ellen Rickey, "Rhymecraft in Edward and George Herbert," *Journal of English and Germanic Philology* 57 (1958): 510.

19. Thurston Dart, "Lord Herbert of Cherbury's Lute Book," *Music and Letters* 38 (1957): 136–48.

Chapter Six

1. Moore Smith, ed. *Poems English and Latin,* 152; but cf. Rossi, *La vita,* 3:389. Diana Cecil may be the model for Celinda in the "Ode" discussed in the next chapter. In that poem Herbert's spokesman bears the name Melander, which means the "black man." Aubrey reports of Edward Herbert, "I have seen him several times . . . he was a black man" (134). And authorship of the sequence of poems in praise of black beauty would certainly have earned Herbert the right to speak as Melander.

2. Hugo Friedrich, *Epoche della lirica italiana,* vol. 3, trans. L. Banfi and G. Bruscaglioni (Milan, 1976), 167–68. Friedrich's excellent annotations to the poem are drawn upon in the following survey of the tradition.

3. *The Greek Anthology,* 5:210 in the Loeb translation by W. R. Paton, vol. 1 (1917), 232–33.

4. André Chastel, *Marsile Ficin et l'art* (1954; reprint, Geneva, 1975), 103–4.

5. John L. Harrison, "Lord Herbert's Two Sonnets on Black," *Notes and Queries* 198 (1953), 323.

6. Donne, "The Storm," v. 67; in *Complete English Poems*, ed. Smith, 198.

7. *The Mystical Hymns of Orpheus*, trans. Thomas Taylor (Chiswick, 1824), 10.

8. Caspar Dornau, *Amphitheatrum Sapientiae Socraticae Joco-Seriae* (Hanover, 1619), 694–718. The Orphic passage is repeatedly echoed by different authors.

9. *The Works of Dionysius the Areopagite*, part 1, trans. John Parker (London, 1897), 130.

10. Ronald E. McFarland, "The Rhetoric of Optics in Lord Herbert's Poems to Diana Cecil," *Medievalia et Humanistica* 5 (1974): 215–28.

11. Ronald E. McFarland, "The Rhetoric of Medicine: Lord Herbert's and Thomas Carew's Poems of Green-Sickness," *Journal of the History of Medicine and Allied Sciences* 30 (1975): 250.

12. McFarland, "Rhetoric of Optics," 223.

13. Heinrich Lausberg, *Handbuch der literarischen Rhetorik*, vol. 1 (Munich, 1960), 183, 511.

14. *Montgomeryshire Collections* vol. 20 (1886), 279.

15. Rossi, *La vita*, 3:5.

16. G. F. Sensabaugh, "Platonic Love and the Puritan Rebellion," *Studies in Philology* 37 (1940): 457.

17. Quoted in G. F. Sensabaugh, "Love Ethics in Platonic Court Drama, 1625–1642," *Huntington Library Quarterly* 1 (1938): 279.

18. Ibid., 280.

19. Rossi, *La vita*, 3:8.

20. Rossi, *La vita*, 3:18.

21. Ibid.; Moore Smith ed., *Poems*, 81, 161.

22. Rossi, *La vita*, 3:246n.

Chapter Seven

1. Alvarez, *School of Donne*, 61.

2. Ellrodt, *Poètes métaphysiques*, 2:15.

3. George Williamson, *Seventeenth Century Contexts* (London, 1960), 72–73.

4. Jefferson Butler Fletcher, *The Religion of Beauty in Woman* (New York, 1911), 191–92.

5. Bruce King, *Seventeenth-Century English Literature* (New York, 1982), 76.

6. Austin Warren, "Donne's 'Extasie,' " *Studies in Philology* 55 (1958): 474.

7. Donne, *Complete English Poems*, ed. Smith, 53–56.

8. *De Causis Errorum*, Gawlick facsim., 1:47.

9. *Dialogue*, Gawlick facsim., 3:141–43.

10. C. J. Fordyce and T. M. Knox, "The Library of Jesus College, Oxford. With an Appendix on the Books Bequeathed thereto by Lord Herbert of Cherbury," *Proceedings and Papers of the Oxford Bibliographical Society* 5 (1937): 97.

11. Fortunat Strowski, *Pascal et son temps*, vol. 1 (Paris, 1909), 161.

12. Ibid., 188–89, 208.

13. Peter Charron, *Of Wisdome* (London, n.d.; facsim. reprint, Amsterdam, 1971), 31–34.

14. Herbert J. Grierson, ed., *Metaphysical Lyrics and Poems of the Seventeenth Century* (Oxford, 1925), 223. Grierson attributes this interpretation to Moore Smith, although the latter did not offer it in his edition.

15. Gordon Williams, "Spiritual Love and Sexual Death in Edward Herbert's Poetry," *Language & Literature* 2 (1974):29; John Hoey, "A Study of Lord Herbert of Cherbury's Poetry," *Renaissance and Modern Studies* 14 (1971):86.

16. *Autobiography*, ed. Lee, 16.

17. *De Veritate*, ed. Carré, 124.

18. On this cycle, see the Latin poems Herbert inserts in his autobiography; Lee ed., 16–18. The only English rendering is that of Margaret Fuller in "The Two Herberts"; see Margaret Fuller Ossoli, *Art, Literature and the Drama* (Boston, 1889), 36–39.

19. *De Veritate*, ed. Carré, 124, 196, 197, 193, 198, 123, 189, 124.

Chapter Eight

1. *Autobiography*, ed. Lee, xii. Further references to this work in the present chapter will be given parenthetically in the text.

2. Cruttwell, *Shakespearean Moment*, 179.

3. Bedford, *Defence of Truth*, 9.

4. Rossi, *La vita*, 3:514.

5. *Autobiography*, ed. Lee, xli.

6. *Horace Walpole's Correspondence*, vol. 35, ed. W. S. Lewis et al. (New Haven, 1973), 452.

7. *The Life of Edward Lord Herbert of Cherbury*, ed. Horace Walpole (Strawberry Hill, 1764), sigs. a2v, b1. The copy used was the beautiful one in the New York Public Library.

8. Rossi, *La vita*, 3:514.

9. Ibid.

10. *The Life of Edward, First Lord Herbert of Cherbury*, ed. J. M.

Shuttleworth (London, 1976), xvii. George Guffey explains why the Lee edition remains preferable; see Guffey's review of Shuttleworth in *Journal of English and Germanic Philology* 78 (1979): 258–61.

11. *The Autobiography of Edward Lord Herbert of Cherbury,* ed. C. H. Herford (Newtown, Montgomeryshire, 1928), vii, viii, xi, x.

12. Margaret Bottrall, *Every Man a Phoenix: Studies in Seventeenth-Century Autobiography* (London, 1958), 73.

13. *Lives of Lord Herbert of Cherbury and Thomas Ellwood with Essays by William D. Howells* (Boston, 1877), 1, 14.

14. Rossi, *La vita,* 3:508–12, 164–69, esp. 167.

15. Stephen, "Lord Herbert," 661; Cruttwell, *Shakespearean Moment,* 179.

16. Rossi, *La vita,* 3:187.

17. Richard Ward, *The Life of . . . Henry More,* ed. M. F. Howard (London, 1911), 147. The book was first published in 1710.

18. Girolamo Cardan, *De subtilitate* (Paris, 1550), 235.

19. *Oeuvres philosophiques de Vanini,* trans. M. X. Rousselot (Paris, 1842), 307–8. Herbert had in his library a copy of the Latin original, *De Admirandis Naturae . . .* (Paris, 1616); see Fordyce and Knox, "Library of Jesus College," 90.

20. See Busson, *La Pensée religieuse française,* 318–49.

21. Lyttle, "Lord Herbert," 251.

22. *De Veritate,* Gawlick facsim., 1:xiv, xliii.

23. *The Major Poems of Timothy Dwight,* ed. W. J. McTaggart and W. K. Bottorff (Gainesville, Fla., 1969), 341.

24. W. K. Jordan, *The Development of Religious Toleration in England,* vol. 2 (1936; reprint, Gloucester, Mass., 1965), 440n.

25. Webb, *Studies in the History of Natural Theology,* 348.

26. *De Veritate,* Gawlick facsim., 1:xv.

27. Rossi, *La vita,* 2:399; Jordan, *Religious toleration,* 2: 440n.

28. Henry Burton, *A Narration of the Life of Mr. Henry Burton* (London, 1643), 12, 24–25, 29.

29. Paul Delany, *British Autobiography in the Seventeenth Century* (London, 1969), 16.

30. Jonathan Goldberg, "Cellini's *Vita* and the Conventions of Early Autobiography," *Modern Language Notes* 89 (1974): 71–83.

Chapter Nine

1. Johannes Musaeus, *Dissertationes Duae* (Jena, 1675), 48–49, 65–66.

2. Baxter, *More Reasons,* 164.

3. Skelton, *Ophiomaches,* 2:312–13.

4. Leland, *A View,* 4–5.

5. Arthur O. Lovejoy, "The Parallel of Deism and Classicism," *Modern Philology* 29 (1932): 281–99.

6. Herbert M. Morais, *Deism in Eighteenth Century America* (New York, 1934), 29–30.

7. Ibid., 66.

8. Westfall, "Isaac Newton's *Theologiae Gentilis,*" 15–34.

9. Gay, *Deism,* 13.

10. Margaret Fuller Ossoli, *Art, Literature, and Drama,* 39.

11. Ibid., 25, 27–28.

12. Ibid., 32–33.

Selected Bibliography

PRIMARY SOURCES

The Autobiography of Edward, Lord Herbert of Cherbury. Edited by Sidney
Lee. London: George Routledge, 1906. Reprint. Westport, Conn.:
Greenwood Press, 1970.
De Religione Gentilium. Amsterdam, 1663. Facsimile reprint. Edited with
an introduction by Günter Gawlick. Stuttgart: Friedrich Frommann,
1967. This is the second volume of Gawlick's edition in facsimile of
Herbert's philosophical writings.
The Antient religion of the gentiles. Translated by William Lewis. London,
1705.
De Religione Laici. Edited and translated by Harold R. Hutcheson. New
Haven: Yale University Press, 1944.
De Veritate. Third edition. London, 1645. Facsimile reprint. Edited with
an introduction by Günter Gawlick. Stuttgart: Friedrich Frommann,
1966. The first volume of Gawlick's facsimile reprinting.
De Veritate. Translated by Meyrick H. Carré. Bristol: University of Bristol,
1937.
A Dialogue between a Tutor and His Pupil. London, 1768. Facsimile reprint.
Edited with an introduction by Günter Gawlick. Stuttgart: Friedrich
Frommann, 1971. The third and final volume of Gawlick's facsimile
edition.
The Expedition to the Isle of Rhé. London: Philobiblon Society, 1860.
The Life and Reign of King Henry the Eighth. With the autobiography.
London: Alexander Murray, 1870.
The Poems English and Latin of Edward Lord Herbert of Cherbury. Edited by
G. C. Moore Smith. Oxford: Clarendon Press, 1923. The standard
edition.

SECONDARY SOURCES

Bedford, R. D. *The Defence of Truth: Herbert of Cherbury and the Seventeenth
Century.* Manchester: Manchester University Press, 1979. The best
book in English on Herbert's thought. Lays stress on Neoplatonic

134

and hermetic elements. Tends to overstate the typicality of Herbert as a man of his age, blunting the critical thrust of his deism.

Ellrodt, Robert. *Les Poètes métaphysiques anglais.* Two parts in three volumes. Paris: Jose Corti, 1960. Regrettably untranslated. The best study of the English metaphysical poets includes a fine chapter on Herbert's verse. Distinguishes Herbert's Platonism as a poet from the incarnational way of apprehending the world of a poet like Donne.

Fordyce, C. J. and T. M. Knox. "The Library of Jesus College, Oxford. With an Appendix on the Books Bequeathed thereto by Lord Herbert of Cherbury." *Proceedings and Papers of the Oxford Bibliographical Society* 5, part 2 (1937):53–115. Some of Herbert's Latin and Greek books. Gives a sense of the wide range of his reading, and of his book collecting.

Fuller [Ossoli], Margaret. "The Two Herberts." In *Art, Literature, and the Drama,* edited by Arthur B. Fuller. Boston: Roberts Brothers, 1889. Dated and sentimental, but one of the few serious efforts to do justice to both Edward and George Herbert.

Hoey, John. "A Study of Lord Herbert of Cherbury's Poetry." *Renaissance and Modern Studies.* 14 (1971):69–89. A competent survey. Stresses the versatility of his poetic talent.

Leland, John. *A View of the Principal Deistical Writers.* London, 1754. Remains a judicious and graceful introduction to Herbert's deism.

Lyttle, Charles. "Lord Herbert of Cherbury, Apostle of Ethical Theism," *Church History* 4 (1935):247–67. Quirky, but independent and at points very insightful. Notes the seriousness of Herbert's *Autobiography* and the artful boldness of the *Dialogue.*

McFarland, Ronald E. "The Rhetoric of Medicine: Lord Herbert's and Thomas Carew's Poems of Green-Sickness." *Journal of the History of Medicine and Allied Sciences* 30 (1975):250–58.

———. "The Rhetoric of Optics in Lord Herbert's Poems to Diana Cecil." *Medievalia et Humanistica,* n.s. 5 (1974): 215–28. McFarland's two essays explore the scientific background of Herbert's poetic imagery. Learned and illuminating.

Merchant, W. Moelwyn. "Lord Herbert of Cherbury and Seventeenth-Century Historical Writing." *Transactions of the Honourable Society of Cymmrodorion* (1956):47–63. An adept brief reading of the tone and intention of the biography of Henry VIII. The best published treatment of Herbert as literary artist.

Popkin, Richard H. *The History of Scepticism from Erasmus to Descartes.* New York: Harper Torchbooks, 1968. Locates Herbert's philosophical endeavors within the overall "sceptical crisis" of the age. The finest book in English on the intellectual background of *De Veritate.*

Rickey, Mary Ellen. "Rhymecraft in Edward and George Herbert." *Journal of English and Germanic Philology.* 57 (1958):502–11. Shows the technical virtuosity of both Herberts. Suggests influence of the older brother upon the younger.

Rossi, Mario M. *La vita, le opere, i tempi di Edoardo Herbert di Chirbury {sic}.* 3 vols. Florence: G. C. Sansoni, 1947. This massive study stands as a lion in the path for students of Herbert. Vastly learned, generally accurate in detail, it offers an excellent account of Herbert's diplomatic career. But Rossi's hostility to deism renders him a very biased judge of Herbert as a man, writer, and thinker.

————. "The Nature of Truth and Lord Herbert of Cherbury's Inquiry." *The Personalist* 21 (1940):243–56, 394–409. The reader without Italian can sample Rossi's diffuse and opinionated writing on Herbert.

Sorley, W. R. "The Philosophy of Herbert of Cherbury." *Mind* 3 (1894):491–508. A useful general account from the standpoint of the history of philosophy.

Stephen, Leslie. "Lord Herbert of Cherbury." *National Review* 35 (1900):661–73. A good statement of the standard hostile view of Herbert as coxcomb—the view that emerged from a misreading of the autobiography.

Webb, Clement C. J. *Studies in the History of Natural Theology.* Oxford: Clarendon Press, 1915. A highly useful survey of the tradition of natural theology (what can be known of God by the light of nature). Concludes with a very readable chapter on Herbert.

Williams, Gordon. "Spiritual Love and Sexual Death in Edward Herbert's Poetry." *Language & Literature* 2 (1974):16–31. The sexual as a figure for the soul's quest for the divine. Eccentric, often simply wrong. But one of the richest general studies in print on Herbert's verse.

Index

Acontius, Jacobus, 21; *Satan's Stratagems,* 21
Allen, D. C., 24, 40–41, 45
Alvarez, A., 66, 95
Anderson, Judith, 65
Aubrey, John, 16

Bacon, Francis, 55–57; *History of the Reign of King Henry VII,* 56–57
Balagny, 110
Baxter, Richard, 117
Bedford, R. D., 19, 33, 35, 104
Bentley, Richard, 24
Blount, Charles, 118
Bottrall, Margaret, 106
Brown, Sir Thomas, 35
Buckingham, duke of, 14, 51–55; expedition to Isle of Rhé, 14, 51–55
Burthogge, Richard, 27
Burton, Henry, 115; and Puritan autobiography, 115
Byrd, William, 4

Camden, William, 4
Carew, Sir George, 6–7
Carré, Meyrick, 18–19
Cassirer, Ernst, 33
Cecil, Diana, 78
Charles I, King, 14, 15, 51, 55, 58
Charon, Pierre, 97; *Of Wisdom,* 97
Cherbury, 1
Cherbury, Edward, Lord Herbert of. *See* Herbert, Edward
Chirbury. *See* Cherbury
Cicero, 37; *De Natura Deorum,* 37
Cleland, James, 7
Collins, Anthony, 118
Collins, Churton, 66
Color, poems on, 78–87
Common Notions, 28–33, 46, 117
Cotton, Sir Robert, 56
Cruttwell, Patrick, 66, 104, 107

Danvers, Sir John, 4
Deism, 2, 13, *22–35,* 44, 45, 57, 63, 94, 97, 117, 118, 119; in Colonial America, 118

Delany, Paul, 115
Dilthey, Wilhelm, 33
Discursive thought, 29–33
Donne, John, 3, 4, 66, 67–71, 75, 78, 79, 94, 95–96, 101, 103; "Ecstasy, The," 95–98; "To Sir Edward Herbert, at Juliers," 17
Dowland, John, 74
Dueling, 6–8, 108–10
Dwight, Timothy, 113; "Triumph of Infidelity, The," 113

"Ecstasy, The" (John Donne), 95–98, 99, 102
Edwards, Jonathan, 23
Elias, Norbert, 7
Eliot, T. S., 66
Elizabeth I, Queen, 3–4, 11, 21
Ellrodt, Robert, 67, 72, 95
Empson, William, 16

Fideism, 20
Fletcher, J. B., 96, 98
Franklin, Benjamin, 118
Fuller, Margaret, 119–20; "Two Herberts, The," 119

Galileo, 33–34
Gawlick, Günter, 47, 49, 50, 114
Gay, Peter, 34–35, 119
Grierson, Herbert J., 99
Grotius, Hugo, 13, 21–22; *De Veritate Religionis Christianae,* 22

Hale, J. R., 55
Hall, Joseph, 5–6
Halyburton, Thomas, 34–35
Henrietta Maria, Queen, 87
Henry Tudor, King, 58–65, 108
Herbert, Edward: ambassadorial years, 10–17, 112; early years, 1–4; as historian, 51–65; as Jacobean, 5, 11; Lord Herbert of Castle Island, Ireland, 13; Lord Herbert of Cherbury, 13; as lutenist, 4, 74; sheriff of Montgomery county, 4; as soldier and lover, 8–10; travels and duels: 1608–1619, 4–10

137

DATE DUE
